DEADLY

DEADLY

DEADLY DIARIES

STEVE BACKSHALL

CONTENTS

SIXTY SPECIES

SIX CONTINENTS

AND SIX MONTHS ON THE ROAD . . .

SIXTY SPECIES, SIX CONTINENTS AND SIX MONTHS ON THE ROAD...

Series Three of Deadly 60 was all about animal record holders. We found the largest animal ever, the biggest toothed predator, the biggest cat, snake, lizard and reptile, the rarest dog, the most venomous snake, octopus and animal of all. We filmed the quickest mammal and fastest fish, the world's longest centipede and the biggest venomous beastie. There were also a whole bunch of firsts for me; swimming with my first gator, free-diving with scintillating sailfish and blue whales, and dangling under a helicopter waiting to be dropped into an occupied crocodile nest!

Getting to grips with a green anaconda.

When I'm on the road I always keep a diary, jotting down every challenge and triumph. It would be a tragedy to experience such adventures, and let the details slip away as the memories fade. Luckily that won't happen, as I've put them all into this book! This is my chance to share those diaries with you. But before we begin, there's something you need to know...

'My name's Steve Backshall, and this is my search for the Deadly 60, that's sixty deadly creatures from around the world, not just animals that are deadly to me, but animals that are deadly in their own world. My crew and I are travelling the planet, and you're coming with me, every step of the way!'

These words have started every Deadly 60 programme over the last few years, and are well chosen. A lot of people assume from the 'Deadly' title that this series is about creatures that are dangerous to human beings. That is the LAST thing it is about. The more I work with so-called dangerous animals, the more it becomes clear that they mean us no harm. In almost every situation, a snake would rather slither quietly away from a human than bite one, and a shark that can clearly see you and knows what you are won't savage you. Even spiders and scorpions only inject their poison into people when they're inadvertently squished in shoes or clothing. The statistics bear this out.

A Brazilian red-rump tarantula.

There are more than seven billion people in the world. All the four hundred and fifty-four species of sharks combined kill only about four people a year, and some years none at all. Last year just two people were reported killed by grizzly bears. Australia has some of the world's most venomous spiders, yet there have been NO recorded deaths from spider bites since antivenoms became available, and there is less than

The endangered Orinoco crocodile.

one death a year there from crocodiles or snake bite. Let's put that into perspective: around twenty-four thousand humans a year are killed by being struck by lightning! More than forty-two thousand are killed in car crashes in the USA alone. The humble mosquito is the only animal on Earth that is a significant killer of human beings due to the diseases it spreads. As many as one and a half million people die from malaria every year.

If I were to make a series about how wild animals are dangerous to human beings, it would be very short indeed!

Filming dolphins hunting for mullet.

THE IDEA

The relationships between predator and prey 'in their own world' are to me the most fascinating aspect of zoology. We're all fascinated by top or apex predators, because they're the fastest, the strongest, the most powerful. They are the masters of their environment.

For biologists, the relationships are even more important. There is good evidence that the continual 'arms race' between species is one of the most important drivers of evolution. The whole act of predation is one of the main reasons our world is so complex, and so exciting. Imagine a hypothetical common ancestor between the leopard and

Cheetah hunting impala.

the cheetah. It probably looked someway between the two modern animals. Over hundreds of thousands of years one cat changed subtly, its skeleton becoming lighter, its spine more flexible, the skull smaller and more streamlined. The chest swelled to accommodate vast lungs and a powerful heart, making it adept at flat-out chases that can last several hundred metres. As the cheetah turned into the natural world's Ferrari, the gazelles it preyed upon had to keep one step ahead, becoming more manoeuvrable, and developing tactics and skills to evade their pursuers.

As this was happening, the leopard was evolving along completely different lines. Its bones became stouter, stronger. Its head got bony and heavy, housing massive jaw muscles that drive a bite to pierce hide and even bone. Now a formidably powerful animal, it is strong

Leopard chasing prey.

enough to withstand the kicks and bites of larger prey that the cheetah cannot risk attacking. However, the leopard is too hefty for sustained chases and needs to creep to within about five metres before pouncing. To stay ahead of the game, its prey animals developed eyes on the sides of their heads, so they had a wider field of vision. They lived together in herds, so that even if one animal had its head down feeding, many other eyes could always be on the lookout and listening for sneaky camouflaged cats.

Leopard.

With the team searching for Bengal tigers in Nepal.

This is massively simplifying the impact of generations of evolution, and the animals themselves had no say in the transformations. But the deal is not done! We still have so much to learn, and nature continues to change. Whales and dolphins are learning new extraordinarily cooperative ways of catching their food (see pages 46 and 191) and while these strategies are as yet confined to small populations of animals, they will surely be passed on to other groups.

Even if the natural world was not changing, it is so infinite in its complexity that you could spend a thousand lifetimes studying it and not know everything, and that's how I like it!

YOU'RE COMING WITH ME ...

This part of the title line means a lot to me – the part about you being with me every step of the way. We've worked really hard on Deadly to develop a way of doing things that is honest, and true to the way things happen. Ever since I started working in television thirteen years ago I've been on a mission to make telly that is as real as possible, and that shows you how it is all done. We've always used a second camera to show us preparing for every shoot, and watching the crew as they do one of the best jobs there is.

Obviously we can't show in real time three days of sitting in a hide, or being out on a boat scouring the seas. All we can do is try our best to give you a sense of how that feels. We aim to have at least one camera rolling all the time, so that when we see something for the first time, you see it too. We're very proud of the fact that in our three series of Deadly which have taken a total of eighteen months on the road filming, we have never cheated, never 'set up' an animal encounter. If we don't find an animal in the wild, we may go and see one in captivity, but we're always totally upfront about that. To me the truth about the natural world is everything.

THE STORIES

My obsession with deadly wildlife means that I am never off duty. Every spare minute is spent on the lookout for great places to film, or gathering contacts and assessing opportunities. At the start of each series I give the team a list of several hundred possible stories, and they have the tough job of making it happen! Not everything will work for us. Each half-hour show is filmed over an average of five days, which is not a lot when you're working with wild animals.

So far our longest shoot was for a UK programme, which needed two weeks of filming thanks to bad weather and animals not showing up. The shortest ever was in Louisiana on Series One, which had to be filmed in two days . . . including an eight-hour drive. Time is tight, so some animals are simply beyond our grasp. Much as I'd like to show you a snow leopard in the high Himalaya, it probably isn't going to happen!

We also need to think carefully about how the programmes are structured. If we are going to film blue whales, which will take at least three days with a high risk that we may not get a sequence, then we need to include at least one other animal in the programme that can be filmed quickly and reliably.

This allows us to take chances, and has had some massive pay-offs over the last year. The inland taipan – probably the most venomous snake in the world – has been seen by very few people in the wild, but we took a gamble, and it paid off with my most satisfying snake encounter ever. Wildlife cameramen told us we were mad to try to film sailfish in the open ocean in just two days, but it resulted in one of the most spectacular shoots ever seen on Deadly. Other wildlife camera crews are still smarting over the fact that we managed to film the rarest dog species on Earth, the Abyssinian wolf, in the mountains of Ethiopia. As with the sailfish, we had just two days to do it, yet still succeeded.

But then again, we've tried three times to find jaguar, and never even seen a footprint!

Filming sand goanna in the Outback.

Sometimes animals are really easy to find, and that has its problems too, a good story shouldn't be too simple. An example would be maned wolves in Brazil. They are rare animals, but we knew they came to be fed at a monastery in the mountains, so we had to think of ways of building up the sequence. To learn more about the wolves, we went out into the wilds around the monastery beforehand and tracked them, following their scat (droppings) and tracks, trying to find out about their prey and their habits. Both we, and hopefully you, will come away knowing more about the animal than if we had simply seen them standing in an electrical storm on the monastery's midnight steps.

THE TEAM

While I may be the one at the sharp end when it comes to catching venomous snakes or handling potentially lethal spiders, it's the crew who have the hardest job. Our team of camera and soundmen are truly hardcore, and I've learned to trust them over many years of expeditions. If you're going to be dangling under a helicopter to be dropped into a crocodile nest, you need to know your wingman is a hundred per cent trustworthy!

Being a cameraman on Deadly is one of the most demanding jobs in television. Johnny, Graham and underwater cameraman Simon have to go everywhere I go, but with a camera on their shoulder that weighs as much as a small child. They have to be able to climb, to scuba dive, to wade through swamps and trudge across deserts, always doing

Preparing to dive a coral reef.

Trying to spot blue whales.

their best to keep the expensive equipment working. They need a sixth sense to be prepared to roll in an instant if a great white shark breaches behind us, or a sparrowhawk unexpectedly hits a pigeon over our heads. Equally, they may have to sit in a hide for days on end, keeping absolutely silent, barely moving, and certainly never falling asleep!

The soundies too are an integral part of the team. All-ears Nick and Smiley Simon are the ears of the programme. I wear a radio microphone, and everything I say is transmitted back to them, then on to the camera. They monitor every bit of the sound, making sure that wind noise, music, engine noises and so on don't blot out what's being said. They are also the heart of our adventures, providing morale, humour and keeping an eye out for danger.

 **YOU'RE COMING WITH ME** 23

Next we have researchers, who help with . . . well, research. They also film with a second smaller camera, which helps to show the good work the rest of the crew are doing. The director completes the line-up. It's their job to edit the programme when we get the footage back to the BBC's Natural History Unit in Bristol, so they keep tabs on where the stories are going, and planning the locations and logistics.

With the crew on the top of Sydney harbour bridge.

Back in the office is an even busier bunch of beavers, from Helena, our calm production manager, who somehow manages to stay on top of the insane amounts of organising, and Scott, the series producer, to the editors, graphics folk and co-ordinators. Together we're like a big fun family, all committed to bringing the best of Deadly to your living room.

DEADLY TECH

On Series Three, we came up with a whole bunch of filming technology to show animal behaviour in new and fresh ways. Some of the results surprised even us!

HIGH SPEED

A conventional camera shoots around twenty-five still frames in a second. As the human eye only sees at about twenty-two frames, when those images are combined we see a continuous moving picture. There are, however, cameras such as the Photron and Phantom that shoot at several hundred, or even thousand, frames a second. The advantage of this is that you can then slow down the footage massively. Animal actions that may be over in a blink or a heartbeat can be appreciated for the first time in super slow-mo. This has had phenomenal results, particularly with sharks and snakes (see pages 66 and 69).

THERMAL

Originally developed by the military, thermal imaging cameras see not with light but with heat. When you look at an image from a thermal camera, cool things come out as blue, warm as orange, and hot as white. They're beautiful and strange, but can have practical uses, both helping us to track animals at night (see page 189) and allowing us to see certain bizarre elements of biology.

INFRARED

Many nocturnal animals are able to see in low light conditions that seem totally black to our eyes, but in complete darkness (for instance, inside a cave) nothing can see. Infrared cameras direct a red light (at a wavelength invisible to human eyes), which illuminate things for the camera. The great thing about this is that it doesn't disturb animals, and allows them to hunt unaware of our presence (see page 130).

MINI-CAMS

Perhaps the biggest development in technology for us has been very small cameras that record great quality images, and can be left running for hours on end. They can be put on kayaks, bikes, planes, even on me. Quite often they'll catch things that we could never hope to react to in time.

BITE TEST GAUGE

At the start of the series, I purchased a pressure gauge with a loop of rubber attached to it. When any animal bit the rubber, the power of its bite was recorded. It's been a great addition to the Deadly kit bag. These are the results we came up with:

Steve Backshall: 140 psi (pounds per square inch)
Spotted hyena: 400 psi
Komodo dragon: 600 psi
Morelet's croc: 800 psi
Alligator: 1000 psi (and then gauge destroyed)
Saltwater croc: 1200 psi (and then gauge destroyed)

These results are . . . unscientific to say the least. To get a proper result, we would need to test the bite of many different animals, and many different times. To find the maximum force you'd need to find the biggest and strongest member of a species, and get them to give their number one bite. The spotted hyena barely nibbled the gauge to register 400 psi, and I'm positive that it could record more than 1000 psi. We'd also need an awful lot stronger gauge!

BACKSHALL'S BOOT CAMP

It'll come as no surprise to anyone who's watched my programmes that I am totally obsessed with being active. Natural chemicals called endorphins are released inside the human body in response to physical activity, sunlight, fresh air and excitement, and I like to make sure I get some of those endorphins flowing round my body every single day. I never know when I'll be called on to scale a towering icefall, or paddle down a raging whitewater river, so I train; sometimes three or four times a day, to make sure I'm always ready.

Since I was very small I've done martial arts like judo and karate, but it can be quite difficult to do those when you're on the road. My favourite things to do are outdoors sports like cycling, mountain biking, rock climbing, kayaking, fell running and mountaineering, as if you keep your eyes and ears open when you're doing them, you're bound to see wildlife. If I can't practically manage those, I'll go to the gym, or do loads of chin-ups, press-ups and a bunch of other funky exercises. Sometimes I convince the whole crew to join me, in a full-on Backshall boot camp! Drop and give me twenty!

Filming in the swamps of Florida.

DEADLY ENVIRONMENTS

Every environment has its own unique challenges for film-makers, and on Deadly we know that better than anyone. On one memorable shoot we flew straight from the Arctic Circle at -30°C to the desert where the temperature was +40°C!

UNDERWATER

Perhaps the worst problems with sub-aqua filming are spending long days on boats, getting seasick and sunburned. There are serious safety concerns once we're in the water though, ranging from the pressure and the chance of running out of air, to the sombre realities of getting tangled in discarded fishing gear or a wreck.

To film underwater we need waterproof housings, which are heavy and cumbersome. I also wear a full-face mask that allows you to see my face, and lets me talk into a microphone so you can hear me.

Preparing to dive in an underground river called a 'cenote' in Mexico.

This series we've filmed some of our most memorable sequences free-diving, or breath-hold diving. This makes us much more manoeuvrable, but does mean the amount of time that we can spend below the waves is very limited. In order to increase the length of my dives I've had to train hard, with breathing and relaxation plans as well as swimming thousands of lengths underwater in the pool! It's paid off though, as nothing makes me feel more free, or more at home in a fish's world than ditching all my hefty scuba kit, and plunging beneath the waves with little more than a mask and a deep, deep breath.

ARCTIC

Chilly conditions are actually very easy to prepare for. Dry cold can be kept at bay with modern fabrics and down clothing. It's much harder to keep warm in a Scottish winter, when it's 5°C and pouring with rain, than in the Arctic Circle when it's -30°C but dry. One nasty side effect of the chill is that battery life is greatly reduced. Sometimes I have to take the batteries off the camera and keep them warm in my pants for a bit before I can film!

DESERT

Often with desert heat the best thing is to do as the animals do and avoid it, filming at night when the wildlife is out and about. Daytime swelter is draining, and we have to make sure to cover up from the sun and drink loads of water.

JUNGLE

The jungle is our best environment for finding animals, but the worst for the camera equipment. Electronics hate humidity, which is pretty much the defining characteristic of the rainforest. We need to set up hotboxes, which have a light bulb inside, to try to drive some of the moisture out of the cameras, and always shake out our boots before putting them on, in case there's a centipede or cockroach inside!

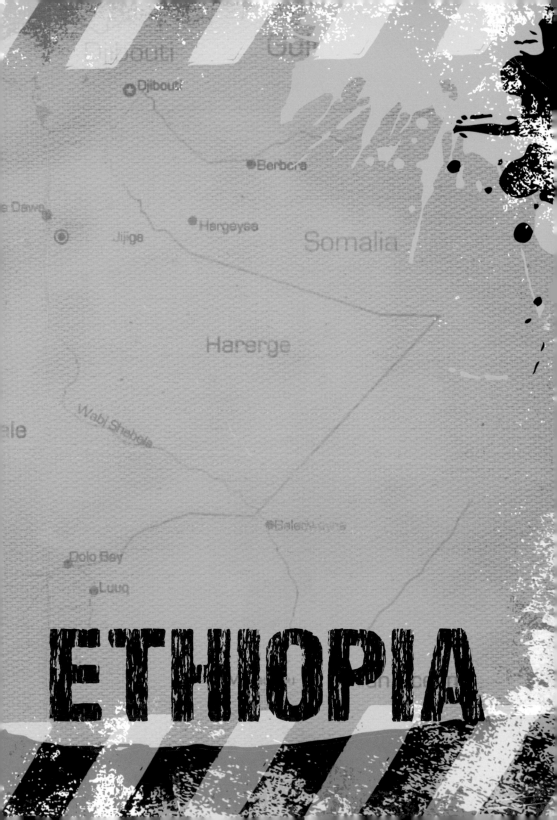

ABYSSINIAN WOLVES (*Canis simensis*)

When deciding where to go first for Series Three, my call was for somewhere we'd not been before so that everything would feel fresh and new. Ethiopia was country number one hundred and one for me, and somewhere I've always wanted to visit. Perhaps the animal that was most enticing was the Abyssinian wolf, but they were also the animal we were too scared to mention. This species of wolf only occurs in the highlands of Ethiopia, but they are so rare that we simply didn't dare to dream we might see one. We were, however, bound for the Bale Mountains on our search for gelada baboons, so I spent four days with my fingers crossed, hoping against hope that we might catch a distant glimpse of a wolf.

There are myriad reasons why these wonderful canids are so endangered. First, they have been ruthlessly hunted by humans, as are all wolves round the world, because they are considered a threat to livestock. More recently they have been horribly affected by diseases such as rabies and mange spread by feral dogs (domestic animals that have escaped into the wild). Their numbers have fallen to about five hundred animals.

These remarkable canids are also known as the Ethiopian wolf, the Abyssinian fox, the red jackal, simien fox or simien jackal. They are smaller than grey wolves and have very different habits. Though they live in loose social groups, they hunt alone, which is really unusual, as

An Abyssinian wolf wandering close to a troop of gelada baboons.

is the fact that males stay with the pack they are born into and it's the females who disperse. As they don't hunt cooperatively, they cannot take large prey. Instead, they feed mostly on rodents such as giant mole rats, creeping up on them before making one final pounce. In order to show how difficult this is, I spent about half an hour creeping up on a mole rat that was sitting in the entrance to its burrow, crawling silently across the grass towards it. The ground was peppered with burrows – there must have been thousands of them. However, as soon as I got within pouncing distance my target sensed me and disappeared.

The Bale Mountains were a wondrous place to film, with dramatic cliff faces dropping hundreds of metres, and vast panoramic views that seemed to go on forever, falling away to the lowlands many kilometres away. The birds of prey were incredibly special. We stood dumbstruck as lammergeiers (also known as bearded vultures) cruised mere metres in front of us, and a pair of saker falcons flew in and out of the nest they'd built on a rugged outcrop a few hundred metres from where we were standing.

At night it got thoroughly chilly due to the altitude, and in our rickety wood-walled hut without a fire or hot water we shivered away, warming ourselves up with cuppa-soups and musty-smelling blankets. We'd brought a small generator to power the batteries that run the cameras, but didn't want to run it into the evenings as it was noisy and would spoil the wonderful peace of the mountains. A near full moon washed the landscape around us with a ghostly white light, making everything impossibly beautiful, even seen through the mist of my hot breath.

We succeeded in our task of filming gelada baboons on the very first afternoon in the mountains. Despite being rare, they were all over the place in massive troops. Once we had them 'in the can', we knew that the next two days would be spent in just one way; searching for wolves. We drove slowly through the mountains, binoculars trained on the slopes around us, desperately hoping for a sighting. The roads were dusty and pockmarked, and I searched them in vain for our canine contender.

On the afternoon of the second day, the jeep screeched to a halt. From the side of the road, trotting nonchalantly, came an elegant red dog, our first Abyssinian wolf! It was total chaos, Graham and I battled to get out of the car as quickly as we could without making any noise and scaring it away. It was a losing battle unfortunately, as the wolf was gone before we could get a decent shot. We followed it across the mountains, but it must have disappeared into a den somewhere. Disconsolate, we headed for home. Next day, though, we hit gold. We were driving very slowly when a voice from the back cried, 'Wolf!'

Filming an Abyssinian wolf - the chance of a lifetime.

This time the wolf was further away, perhaps a hundred metres from us, wandering lazily through an alpine meadow where hundreds of geladas were grazing. He was unaware or uninterested in us, and was merrily strolling around, so Graham took the time to get out his super-big lens and tripod, and set up to film at a distance. I watched fascinated through my binoculars, as this impossibly rare, utterly beautiful dog prowled between tussocks. I turned to the second camera, to do a piece about the wonder we were witnessing.

'Abyssinian wolves creep along the ground, before making one final leap on their prey.' As I finished talking, Graham looked up at me sharply.

'You know what you just said?' Gray stuttered, flummoxed. 'It just happened! While you were talking about it!'

And when we watched the footage back that's exactly what had occurred. Almost as if I was a football commentator talking about a great goal, I described the wolf prowling forward and then leaping on to a rodent and scoffing it. Pure chance of course, but rather poetic just the same, and one of the more memorable and important encounters of my career.

The wolf preparing to pounce on a rodent.

PIED KINGFISHER (*Ceryle rudis*)

Lake Tana is Ethiopia's largest lake, and a sensational place for birdlife. Here we had many predatory birds to choose from. Marabou storks had been our original idea, but they are almost entirely scavengers. I managed to convince an African fish eagle to snatch fish from the lake in front of us which got my vote, but we'd filmed them on Series

One so kept our options open. Finally, back at the lakeshore, we watched pied kingfishers hovering before plummeting into water that was perilously shallow, almost always emerging with a fish in their beaks. Their hovering was so expert and their success rate so high that we decided they'd be our winner.

GELADA BABOON (*Theropithecus gelada*)

Geladas were a difficult one for this series. We couldn't go to Ethiopia without filming these rare, endemic (which means they only occur here), mountain-living monkeys. It's easy to justify filming most baboons as they occasionally prey on other animals, but geladas are strict herbivores. However, they do have canine teeth that are as long as a lion's and have been known to attack leopards and hyenas that threaten their families, and that is good enough for me!

Watching a troop of gelada baboons.

SPOTTED HYENA (*Crocuta crocuta*)

There's much that's unusual about the biology of spotted hyenas. First they have matriarchal, that is female-controlled, clans, and the girls are much bigger and meaner than the boys, which is very unusual for mammals. They also probably have one of the most powerful bites of all mammals, as they have a broad, blunt snout, with stout carnassial (cheek) teeth that deal with bone like nutcrackers deal with feeble hazelnuts.

We went to an ancient walled city where the local people had been feeding hyenas for generations, and sat in darkness with a man who knew every animal by name, and fed them chunks of meat by hand. It was pretty scary; I've seen hyenas driving lions off their prey, and here they were prowling casually around us, snatching meat from the bucket at our feet, and crunching through sinew and bone with sickening sounds. Though I never quite conquered my nervousness, it was an awe-inspiring encounter.

I get as close as I dare to spotted hyenas.

Nome

Wade
Hampton

Bristol Bay

Aleutians East

GRIZZLY BEAR (*Ursus arctos horribilis*)

From the scorching lowlands and verdant mountains of Ethiopia, the crew and I journeyed to one of my favourite wildlife destinations on the planet. Alaska can be brutal in the winter, and much of the north is inside the Arctic Circle. The south of the state though is lush, covered with pine and spruce forests, with glassy lakes framed by snow-capped peaks. Flying over the state you can travel for hours and all you see below is wilderness, unclimbed mountains, rivers that have never been run, landscapes without roads. I adore it.

A female grizzly and her cub.

Alaska's most famous animal is the grizzly bear. The brown bear, *Ursus arctos,* is distributed widely throughout the northern hemisphere; grizzly is the name given to brown bears that live in western North America. They are fearsome beasts, and a true deadly icon. It's often said that they can run as fast as a racehorse, 55 km/h, or even 65 km/h. I've encountered grizzly bears many times, but this time was especially rewarding, as it so nearly didn't happen.

We were due to be flying out to an incredibly remote part of the Alaskan coastline only accessible by float-plane. For three days we tried and failed, the weather closing in on us at the last minute. One time we got the plane to within a kilometre or so of camp, before thick fog made us turn back. From there on it was a really scary flight. Being in dense cloud not able to see anything is fine on a modern jet with all its technology, but in a light aircraft when you rely on what you can see, it's terrifying; we didn't know if the visibility would even allow us to land back in town. At the last minute there was a chink in the clouds and we chanced a landing, leaving cameraman Johnny and me very relieved indeed.

Finally I decided we couldn't risk waiting any longer and started asking around to see if anyone knew an alternative location to reliably find bears. One place kept cropping up, a river that was supposedly full of salmon, where bears were regularly seen. We managed to hire a battered old van, with a hole in the floor that you could see the road through; it looked as if it wouldn't get us to the end of the street! Clunking through the gears, we set off on the eight-hour drive inland towards the river.

At last we crossed a bridge over a fast-flowing emerald-clear river, and there was instantly a very good sign. Not bears, but hundreds of fishermen lining the banks. They were there for the salmon, which were running so that you could practically walk across the river on their backs. In Alaska, where you find salmon, you find bear.

Grizzlies are true omnivores. For much of the year they'll eat berries and other fruit, plus insects and their larvae – not what you might expect from one of the world's most awe-inspiring predators. They will chase down deer and other mammal prey, but in midsummer, when the rivers are full of salmon returning to

the rivers they were born in to spawn, that's when bears are at their predatory best.

We hiked along a forest trail for several kilometres to a waterfall that we'd been told might be a good spot for a stake-out. When we got there, I found what looked like the poured out filling from a blueberry pie, with some chunks of seeds and fish scales littered through it . . . grizzly poo, and very fresh! The crew watched in disgust as I pulled it apart with my fingers, and lifted up bits to my nose as if it was chocolate sauce; I've become a bit immune to the yuck factor of animal poo! On the other side of the river tracks were visible, and the water itself was so stacked with salmon I could have hopped in and caught one with my bare hands! The whole place felt like an arena where we would surely find our hulking hero. We sat down super-quietly, and waited.

Taking a break by the river while watching for bears.

Shortly after dusk, shadows filled the canyon we were hiding in, and Johnny was starting to fret about whether we'd have enough light left to film. He informed us that we had no more than twenty minutes left to get our sequence. Everyone looked grim. We'd worked so hard and been so resourceful, surely we couldn't still fail? But fate was kind. Ferns on the slope in front of us rustled and parted, and a large female grizzly ambled easily down to the water's edge; followed by two tiny, tiny cubs. They would have been born that winter in the bear's den, and would stay by her side for at least another year, until big enough to fend for themselves properly. For now though they were beach-ball sized bundles of fuzz, impossibly cute, falling over their own massive paws, and totally incapable of looking after themselves.

The grizzly family fish for salmon.

Mum though did not have that problem. She leapt straight into the waterfall with a titanic belly flop, sending water crashing everywhere, and emerged victorious with a metre-long pink salmon. She put one mammoth paw on top of it, took the head in her mouth, and with barely a twitch ripped the meat off the bone. It was effortless. She filleted the fish with such ease that it set us all thinking about what she could do to us if it took her fancy. She was, after all, no more than five metres away, with only the stream between us. We needn't have worried. Our mamma bear only had fish on the brain. Six times she leapt into the waterfall, emerging like a gargantuan, soaking-wet labrador, and every time she had a huge salmon twitching in her giant jaws. The cubs happily munched away at the scraps, in between rolling around with each other, playing comfortably in this time of plenty. In years to come they would have to cope with hard times; they'd be driven away by their mum and have to fend for themselves, enduring the bitter cold of Alaskan winters, perhaps having to evade hunters' bullets and bows. But for now life was easy, provided for by one of the most expert and well-equipped fishermen imaginable.

Getting up close to a sea otter.

HUMPBACK WHALE
(*Megaptera novaeangliae*)
Humpback whales in Alaska have learned a dramatic way of hunting, called bubble-net feeding. These often solitary animals

come together in big groups of fifteen or more, and swim beneath shoals of herring. One circles around below them, blowing out bubbles from its blowhole, forming a shimmering corral around the fish. The other whales then erupt to the surface, taking in mouthfuls of water and herring as they emerge.

SEA OTTER (*Enhydra lutris*)

Sea otters are the smallest marine mammal, with the most densely packed hair of any creature – perhaps a hundred thousand hairs per

square centimetre. This gives them great insulation, and they're continually grooming themselves to keep a layer of air underneath the fur, which then warms up with their body heat. Sea otters dive down to the seabed to collect prey like clams and crabs, which they bring to the surface to break open. They put a rock on their chest (kept in a pouch in their armpit), then smash the food open on it, making them one of very few animals to use tools.

WEASELS

One family of animals has had disproportionate representation on Deadly 60, as it includes some of the feistiest, most aggressive of creatures. It's the family Mustelidae, more commonly known as the weasels. We've featured the wolverine; no bigger than a collie dog and with much shorter legs, it's been known to take down moose! And honey badgers make the *Guinness Book of Records* as the most fearless animals on Earth; they'll drive hyenas and even lions away from their prey. Giant river otters totally rule their Amazonian home rivers, even killing fully-grown crocs and anacondas. Otters, stoats, martens, badgers, skunks, mink and, of course, our sea otter, are brave, bright and consistently punch above their weight. Mustelids. Marvellous!

A sea otter in Alaskan waters.

Scotland

GREAT
BRITAIN

Wales

DRAGONFLY (Order Odonata)

One of my fond beliefs is that adventure starts at home. Rather than always lusting after the exotic, it's essential that we take pride in the wildlife that inhabits our backyards, and my backyard is Great Britain. My home country may not have taipans or tiger sharks, and we exterminated all our wolves, bears and lynx eons ago, but it still has wild wonders to match any place on Earth.

A four-spotted chaser dragonfly.

A dragonfly sits happily on my finger.

Dragonflies are for me the perfect Deadly 60 animal. Incredibly fast, manoeuvrable, totally unstoppable predators in their own world, but absolutely no danger to human beings. We have thirty-seven species here in the UK, and Wicken Fen in Norfolk is a great place to go looking for them, in among the reed beds and ponds. I caught several dragonflies in my butterfly net, in order to film their flight in super-slow motion. It was breathtaking, seeing them take off like helicopters, rising vertically with circular motions of their wings.

CONGER EEL (*Conger conger*)

British waters play host to some mighty marine beasts, including minke whales, orca, the largest bottlenose dolphins in the world, grey and common seals and sharks such as blues, makos, threshers and porbeagles. However, you'd have to go a long way to find anything as creepy as the mighty conger eel. European congers are the largest eels in the world, and can grow to be truly mammoth; as much as three metres in length and much more than my bodyweight. I've always filmed them quite close to shore, but they're known to live at over one thousand metres down, in perpetual darkness.

Our location was in the middle of Plymouth Sound, a busy shipping lane full of ancient wrecks and a hotspot for UK diving. I'd done my

Diving in search of conger eels.

commercial diving qualifications here, and knew the waters well; they're always chilly, sometimes low on visibility, but can offer some of the most rewarding diving in southern England. At first, our dive site seemed far from ideal. Being in the middle of a busy shipping lane meant that whenever we were underwater the chaps up top needed to be vigilant for the approach of supertankers and fishing boats! Secondly, it was a very little known dive site. Locals told tales of a monstrous conger eel that had been spotted within the engine block of a much-dilapidated wreck.

We seemed to be going purely on myth and legend, and that is never a good idea. It seemed that we could easily spend all day and night diving in freezing waters without seeing anything; Johnny and I were sceptical to say the least! In order to coax out a conger if one was lurking inside the wreck, I took down a porous bag filled with smelly sardines, as well as another bag full of fresh whole mackerel. As congers are nocturnal, we didn't expect to see anything by day but figured we might as well go down and have a look, even if it only counted as a recce.

Johnny and I kitted up under blue skies; it was unusually warm for early spring in the UK. The water though was still winter cold, so we wore dry suits – a scuba suit that keeps you relatively dry inside. Unfortunately, some icy water will always run down the back of your neck, and you can't keep your head and face dry, so within minutes of getting in we were longing for a hot shower and a nice cuppa. The two of us dropped down to the site of the wreck. It was nothing special. The engine block was about the size of half a squash court, with no recognisable features. There were a few pollack hanging around in one of the alcoves, but not much else. If we didn't find any congers, this would be the shortest sequence we'd ever filmed for Deadly.

When I've filmed congers before, my plan has been to waft the bag of stinky fish over the hole where the eel is supposed to be. Congers have extraordinary senses of smell and taste, with two extra tubular nostrils just above their upper lip. They zone in on any flavour molecules in the water, so allowing scents to trickle out of the bag is a great way to tantalise them and get them into the open.

Unbelievably, almost instantly a conger tail lashed out of the engine block. It hadn't just been a myth! This one was no giant, but it was certainly a start. For the moment it was cautious, but we considered it a good sign, and headed up to the surface, preparing to dive again as soon as it got good and dark.

After nightfall filming was a totally different story. Once we'd hung the bag of smelly fish outside the hole, our first small conger came

A conger comes close to investigate.

right into the open. Its attitude was completely different; it swam actively between my legs, and then snapped at my bubbles. I think this was down to the conger's ropy eyesight mistaking my bubbles for the shimmering scales on a small fish.

We'd got some wonderful footage, and were thinking of returning to the boat, when something monstrous loomed out of the wreck. This was the biggie they'd been talking about. It didn't come fully into the open, but far enough to snatch whole fish from my hands, sucking them down in one like a giant vacuum cleaner. At this size, it had to be a female; its head was bigger than mine and it must have been two

We find a huge two metre conger!

metres in length. It was quite a creepy-looking beast, and I took great care not to allow it too near my fingers, but what a creature; and right here in British waters! The cuppa and the hot shower later on were about the sweetest I've ever had!

KESTREL (*Falco tinnunculus*)

The kestrel was once the UK's most common bird of prey, but suffered terribly from the use of pesticides such as DDT, which thinned the shells of the birds' eggs and had a catastrophic effect on their breeding success. Now buzzards and sparrowhawks are both more common, but the kestrel is still a regular sight, hovering over the verges of our motorways. They also have a wonderful set of deadly skills; the ability to see into the ultraviolet spectrum allows them to locate the urine trails left behind by voles as they forage, and their keen eyesight enables them to pinpoint the tiniest movements from shy and tiny prey.

I attempt to hover like a kestrel inside the world's largest vertical wind tunnel.

CHEETAH (*Acinonyx jubatus*)

We were set to film two programmes in South Africa, which makes it equal top Deadly destination with Great Britain and Australia. It has all the big game of East African nations like Kenya and Tanzania, but also has a phenomenally wild coastline, which is the best place in the world for filming sharks. We've filmed there so many times over the years that I've made some great friends, and know people there who make our job incredibly easy.

I meet a captive cheetah.

The fastest mammal on Earth was an obvious choice for this series, particularly as it engages in one of the most spectacular hunts imaginable. Only problem is that a cheetah may go for days without even trying to hunt, and we had just two days.

After we found our pair of cheetahs, we stayed on their tails as they paced their territory, sitting out in blazing sun while they lazed in the shade, desperate to see them leap into action. We had been waiting, totally silent, barely moving for eight long hours, when finally a herd of gazelles moved into view, partially hidden by the undergrowth. Instantly the two cheetahs got to their feet, and began to slink forwards, preparing to hunt. We didn't even dare breathe we were so scared of putting them off their stride. Just as they started to prowl forwards, a tourist jeep roared up – the first we had seen in two days – scaring the gazelle away with their engine. The cheetah slumped back into the shade where they would remain till nightfall. It was a truly miserable moment!

PUFF ADDER (*Bitis arietans*)

For our big African snake sequence we had been given the use of a super-fancy, high-speed camera called a Photron. This wonderful bit of machinery can be used to slow reality right down, so that a second of real time can seem to last an eternity, and things that happen too fast for the human eye to appreciate can be seen in crystal clear close-up. My plan was to gather a snake from each of the three families of venomous snakes, and show one element of their behaviour at high speed.

We hooked up with my old friend and snake specialist, Donald Strydom, who is one of the people I respect most in the world when it comes to serpents. Don is known for miles around as the person to contact if someone finds an unwanted slitherer on their property, and it wasn't long before we got a phone call. A local family had seen something head behind a plant pot on their front porch. They didn't expect to see us rock up with the film cameras rolling, but were quite understanding, and allowed us to film the whole thing.

The description they'd given us perfectly matched the mfezi, or Mozambique spitting cobra. This snake is to my mind the most efficient spitter of all snakes, propelling a jet of venom with staggering accuracy easily two metres towards the eyes of a threat. If this gets into your eyes it causes phenomenal pain, and can blind you, so Don and I wore protective glasses as we moved the pot aside. I knew instantly that we had a mfezi, as I was peppered with venom, which covered my goggles. Gently I put the snake into a bin with a lockable lid, wrote 'Danger: venomous snake' on the side, and headed off in search of more.

Next we pulled up at a farm where the owner said two black mambas had been seen. We approached the bush where he'd seen them very slowly, and from a distance of about sixty metres I scanned the area with my bins. There they were! They were about three and a half metres long, and spread out in the branches. However, as soon as we tried to get any closer they vanished. We came back twice, but every time the same thing happened. So much for a killer snake that chases people trying to bite them!

Next we went bush-bashing, in search of two other species I had in mind. We spent hours in fantastic habitats, and found bugs and spiders, but alas, no snakes. At the end of the day, we gathered dry chunks of wood, and built a fire under a full moon. Fire lighting in damp places can be really frustrating and hard work, especially when you're cold and wet and desperate for warmth. Here though, the wood was bone dry, and leapt into flames with ease. Our biggest concern was ensuring that the sparks didn't carry to nearby scrub (and next morning we had to take great care to make sure not a single glowing ember remained, as it might have started a serious bushfire). Once the fire had burned down sufficiently, we scraped away some of the fiery embers, and made a fire pit, over which we cooked juicy steaks and jacket spuds.

While the others sat chatting around the hypnotic dancing flames, I went out on a last desperate foray for snakes, splashing my headlight into every crack and crevice, patrolling dry riverbeds, and scanning the trees for arboreal (which means living in trees) snakes. After a few hours I gave up; the night was too cool for reptile activity. This time though, I put my head down under the stars knowing we had a back-up plan. Donald runs a snake park, and the following day had some snakes on standby to help us with our experiment.

Venomous snakes come in three families. Elapids (cobras, mambas, taipans, coral snakes, etc) have stout, fixed, short fangs at the front of the upper jaw. Their venoms tend to focus on the nervous system, the heart and the lungs. They're active hunters that go out looking for food. Vipers (adders, sidewinders, pit vipers, rattlesnakes) have hinged, long, hollow fangs at the front of the upper jaw. Their venoms are often complex, but tend to hit the blood and circulatory system. They usually ambush predators that sit still, waiting for prey to come close, and striking quickly towards it. The last group is more tricky. Colubrids (twig snakes, vine snakes, keelbacks) are usually not venomous – or not so that we humans would notice anyway. If they have fangs they're on the upper jaw, but halfway back, and they're grooved not hollow.

The elapids were represented by the mfezi. I wanted to show its spitting prowess in high speed. Donald placed the snake under a small cover, then when it had settled down, removed the cover, and I instantly moved towards it in a threatening manner. The snake flinched momentarily, then unloaded a gush of venom towards my face. I felt the droplets hitting my lips and nose, but the lion's share (an aptly-chosen phrase, as the mfezi in the wild would be spitting at a predator like a lion) was on the goggles right where my eyes were. When we watched the footage slowed down, the results were remarkable. The 'flinch' of the mfezi was actually the snake bringing

Mfezi or Mozambique spitting cobra.

its head back so that its eyes were level with my own, essentially 'sighting' its target. Then the venom came out, not just in a squirt as if out of a pinched hosepipe, but in spiralling streams. The fangs have a twist to the hollow centre, just like the grooves on a gun barrel. This gives the jets better penetration through the air.

Next up was our colubrid, and for this I'd chosen the boomslang, one of the few snakes in this group that could kill a human being. It's very

I get to grips with a boomslang.

unlikely as they're quite placid snakes, but it has happened – everyone assumed boomslangs were not venomous at all until a well-known scientist was handling one, got bitten and dropped down dead. The thing that excites me about boomslangs, though, is their senses. They hunt for extremely well-camouflaged prey like chameleons up in the top of trees, and have superlative eyesight. My idea was simply to film the boomslang's serpent tongue flicking out – something you see all the time with snakes, but never really appreciate. The results were, to me, breathtaking. As the tongue came out of the snake's mouth, it acted almost like a separate animal. The two forks waved around in the air, soaking up smelly scent molecules, then drew them back into the mouth where they could be processed in a special place in the roof of the mouth called the Jacobsen's organ. Then the tongue whipped out again, and wiped itself repeatedly down the branch the snake was lying on, sponging up smelly substances and taking them back in to be analysed. It was stunning.

The viper was easy. We had a puff adder, which is said to be the fastest striking snake on Earth, so obviously I wanted to see it strike! Vipers will strike towards warm objects as if they're prey, so I filled a water balloon, and dangled it in front of our snake. The balloon exploded. It happened so quickly I wasn't even sure that the snake had struck at it, but when we saw it slowed down there was no doubt. The snake extended perhaps a third of its body length towards its target, and as it unfurled, its top jaw flipped back, and the hinged fangs swung up into a stabbing position. The snake punctured the balloon, and carried on moving, the momentum of its strike was so extreme. For a second the water droplets within the balloon hung, suspended in time, glinting with sunlight, before splashing all about our retreating serpent. It is one of the most beautiful shots that I've ever seen. As Johnny the cameraman had done such an incredible job with the filming, I gave him the choice of which snake should make it on to the list, and he had no hesitation. Puff adder, deadly!

GREAT WHITE SHARK (*Carcharodon carcharias*)

The seas off South Africa's coast are legendary for sharks: tigers, makos, raggies, silkies, bronze whalers and, of course, the epitome of what Deadly is all about – an icon among predators, the great white shark. We've attempted to film great whites on Deadly before, and in South Africa too. Last time, the weather beat us. Strong seas and winds meant we didn't have a chance to get in the water with them. This time though I had a different idea about how to show this grand predator at its epic best. Around the world, the majority of great whites' diet is made up of fish, but there are places where they specialise in feeding on mammals. Dyer Island is one such a place. It's home to sixty thousand Cape fur seals, which play and frolic unaware, in a strait between the island and Danger Point on the mainland. The strait has come to be known as Shark Alley.

Watching a great white shark from the safety of a diving cage.

The fur seals themselves are no slouches. They're big, fast, almost balletic predators, and have impressive gnashers, as well as a thick layer of blubber, which is intended for insulation, but can function almost like a sort of suit of armour. For the sharks to take a seal, they need to rely on the element of surprise, and they need to hit the seal very hard indeed. When a shark detects the kind of vibrations at the surface created by a gambolling seal, it swims down deep, then powers

The awesome great white shark.

upwards almost vertically, hitting the seal. The momentum it has built is so great that the shark breaches clear out of the water, aiming to have the seal in its mouth as it does so. The intention is to inflict mortal injuries almost instantaneously in order to kill the seal outright.

Our chances of filming this happening were slim to none. After all, the seal is generally swimming happily with no hint whatsoever of impending danger, before this explosive force from the deep blows it out of the water. We could sit with our cameras on one seal for weeks and not see it happen. However, there is a trick that you can use to try and see a breach kill – we made a seal decoy by wrapping a bunch of polysterene floats in black rubber. The boat then chugged through the prime shark spot, dragging our seal decoy along behind on a length of tough fishing line. The mock-up created the same vibrations as a real seal, and Johnny could focus our high-speed camera on the decoy. If something happened, I would have to press the fire button at exactly the right moment to get our high-speed shot and see the whole thing happening blow by blow.

We headed out at first light. Our boat was big and powerful, but even so, driving through the waves was pretty hairy. It's not just the presence of the most feared animal on the planet that makes these seas frightening. The waves have come all the way from Antarctica, the waters are cold and forbidding and conditions can be horrendous. We still managed to get out to the island not long after sunrise, and what we saw absolutely took our breath away.

Without warning, a melee rent the water not fifty metres from the side of the boat. A shark had hit a seal, and the drama was playing out right in front of our eyes. The first breach attack had not been decisive, and the seal was now battling for its life, leaping, twisting and turning, as the great white's mighty tail thrashed the water into foam. Several times it seemed that the seal leapt right through the shark's mouth, evading those three hundred serrated teeth by a whisker. The crew were enthralled, some I guess willing the seal to make a safe escape, others wanting to witness the triumph of one of the greatest predators that has ever graced our planet.

Johnny, Nick and I scrambled around the boat struggling to find the best vantage point to film from, while taking great care to hang on to the guard rails as the boat pitched and tossed. Knowing what was happening in front of us, nobody wanted to get hurled overboard! Johnny and Nick are best friends, and always watch each other's backs. As Johnny filmed, his eyes pressed to the viewfinder, Nick gripped him round the waist in a bear hug, making sure he knew he was safe. It was a surreal sight in the golden dawn light! The battle seemed to continue for an eternity, but ultimately the seal's agility paid off, and the shark gave up, disappearing into the depths. This was a fantastic sign for us though, and we got our decoy into the water as quickly as we could.

From here on in, it was Johnny who had the hard job. He had to stand on a tossing and turning boat, keeping his camera trained on a decoy he could barely see that was bouncing along perhaps thirty metres behind the boat. Considering he would only have two mornings to get the shot, none of us was holding out much hope.

The shark goes for the decoy seal.

But then, after no more than half an hour, the sea behind us erupted. A shark had hit the decoy! I pressed the button in time, Johnny was trained on the right spot; all we had to do now was wait for the computers to put the slowed down image together. The whole crew crowded around the laptop screen to see the results. They were spectacular. The shark didn't completely clear the water, but we saw perhaps five tonnes of mammoth fish smashing through the surface, chomping on the fake seal for all it was worth. It was a beautiful shot.

Johnny managed to get three more shots afterwards, all slightly different, but each in its own way incredibly dramatic. All we were missing was one where the shark completely cleared the water. Johnny is Northern Irish, with a great sense of humour and bags of energy and enthusiasm. However, like all cameramen he is a perfectionist, and is also quite competitive. One of his fellow cameramen, filming legend Simon King, had managed to get the perfect shot of a shark fully breaching (admittedly after two full weeks at sea) and Johnny didn't want to give up until he'd done at least as well!

A huge great white takes us by surprise.

Towards the end of the second morning of filming, we'd just had one unsuccessful attempt, and Johnny was busy setting up the camera ready for another go. While he was sorting it out, one of the crew members threw the decoy overboard. Every single one of us watched it going in, and thought to ourselves, 'We should bring that in, it would be awful if a shark breached now, and Johnny couldn't film it.' But none of us said anything. It floated behind the boat for about thirty seconds, and then BOOM! The sea erupted with leaping shark.

The shark was the biggest we'd seen, much closer than any of the others. It was lit by the morning sun and had breached completely clear of the water. We were speechless. Johnny looked at us all in total disgust.

The story wasn't over. We got into the water in a specially designed cage, and shot some glorious underwater footage of the sharks. However, the cage also became an unexpected haven, shortly after we'd watched another shark trying to catch a real seal at the surface. The young seal escaped and a few minutes later, turned up inside our shark cage! We were unsure what to do; he was clearly taking refuge from the killers beyond, and I don't blame him, there were three four-metre-long whites circling our boat. He had some teeth wounds on his flippers, wasn't too badly injured, but was clearly exhausted. We couldn't push him out, he'd be munched. We also couldn't pick him up with our hands, because seals have a wicked bite.

After about ten minutes of hoping he'd make a break for freedom himself, we decided to take the boat over to nearby kelp beds, drive as close to them as we dared, and then shoo him out of the cage. For a while he looked as if he would dash for safety, but then he'd bottle out and swim straight back in. Finally he darted off, with a boatful of friends cheering his survivor's spirit, as if we were cheering home the winner of the Tour de France.

THREAT TO SHARKS

Sharks are the most misunderstood beasts on Earth. They pose little or no danger to people, yet we fear them and persecute them. The main threat to their survival comes in the form of shark finning; catching the animals and chopping off their fins, before returning them, dying, to the sea. The fins are used in shark fin soup, a traditional Chinese dish often served at weddings. Because of this, as many as seventy-three million sharks are removed from our seas every year. In some areas shark numbers are down by ninety-nine per cent, and if you take a top predator out of an ecosystem there are massive negative consequences, most likely with an explosion of the creatures they normally feed on.

BUFFALO (*Syncerus caffer*)

Cape buffalo are one of the few non-predatory animals that made it on to the Deadly list, but certainly deserve their spot. These huge bovids (members of the cow family) are reliably grumpy, given to charging at anything they take a dislike to. They'll drive lions away, sometimes even killing them with their mighty horns. Walking into a mammoth herd of buffalo was pretty scary stuff. First we went for a recce in a light aircraft, scouring the horizon for a herd, then went in on foot. This was old-fashioned tracking, paying close attention to the wind direction as it would carry our scent and sounds towards the buffalo. The first time we got to within about fifty metres before the ground reverberated with the rumble of stampeding hooves and the

Part of a herd of Cape buffalo.

buffalo were gone. Second time we got to just a stone's throw from the animals, who stood regarding us balefully before we bid a respectful retreat, quite happy to be heading back to camp.

CROWNED EAGLE (*Stephanoaetus coronatus*)

The crowned eagle is the African equivalent of the Latin American harpy eagle, which catches monkeys in the tree canopy. It's a massive bird, as we found when we got to grips with a captive one in a sanctuary. Its talons were incredibly impressive. Whereas a fish-catching osprey has thin, curved claws like a twisted knitting needle, the crowned eagle has to punch through

Filming a magnificent crowned eagle.

fur and hide, so its talons are stout, sturdy and as thick as my thumb. However, the greatest treat was seeing them in the wild. We had a tip-off about a nest that had been used for many years, and as it was early nesting season decided we should stake it out. The nest was in the mountains, in a huge emergent tree (one higher than all other trees around it) with views down the valley towards potential hunting grounds. As we watched, first the male then the female returned to the nest, and though they had no prey, we did get to watch them mating nearby, which was a rare privilege.

SECRETARY BIRD (*Sagittarius serpentarius*)

The secretary bird is a real animal oddity. It looks a bit like an eagle that has been put on the medieval torture instrument, the rack, and had its legs stretched. These great long legs allow it to strut about above tall grasses on the lookout for prey. That can be anything from bugs to hares, but often includes the most venomous snakes.

To test out how this works, we visited a bird sanctuary where they had a young rescued bird. We had a plastic snake on a line, and aimed to see how the bird would react to it. The second I threw down the snake near to him, the bird stalked over and stamped, straight on the snake's head. He then proceeded to stomp the thing into the dirt, stamping over and again with his tough feet and long, curved claws, every kick a powerful directed blow, and always a bullseye straight to the head. It was remarkable to watch, even more so as the bird had never seen another secretary bird, and its parents had died before he was old enough to learn anything from them. The behaviour must be what's known as 'innate', that is, something you're born with.

KOMODO DRAGON (*Varanus komodoensis*)

It was over fifteen years ago in my early days as a writer that I saw my first Komodo dragon. I was writing a guidebook to Indonesia, and went to Komodo Island three times. One night I sat out with a flashlight on my own, next to a bag of rotten fish guts, and nearly frightened myself to death when the big dragons arrived. Another time a dragon that seemed to be slumbering in a wallow leapt out at a tourist who was getting too close, and ate his camera. I thought I knew this animal and how to read them. I was wrong.

Komodos were the animal that convinced me to do a third series of Deadly 60, as to my mind they were the most obvious omission from previous programmes. They are the largest lizard on Earth, big males growing to almost three metres long and one hundred and fifty kilograms in weight. They're also the biggest venomous animal. Research by Dr Bryan Greig Fry of Melbourne University showed they have true venom glands on the lower jaw that secrete toxins over the frighteningly sharp teeth. This explains why when Komodos bite big prey, such as a fully-grown water buffalo, the animal will eventually succumb though the bite may be small. It may take many weeks for the venom to have its lethal effect.

The crew and I journeyed in an old-fashioned fishing boat, spending the evenings playing cards out on deck by candlelight, and waking super-early to leap overboard and have a wash in the toasty tropical

My close encounter with a Komodo dragon.

sea. At night we slept in a muggy cabin, sweltering hot in the early
evening, then deeply chilled as the damp ocean winds swept through
in the middle of the night. Poor Smiley Simon, the soundie, thought
he'd chosen a prime sleeping spot up on deck until about 1.00 am
when the sea breeze soaked him to the skin and left him shivering
and sleepless. The seas around Komodo are tempestuous, as the tides
rise and fall enormous quantities of water pour between the islands,
forming currents, eddies and whirlpools that can take a boat down
into the depths. The islands themselves have stark cliff faces that seem

to have been rent by the claws of some ancient monster, and are lined with spindly palms and dense bush. It is a fitting prehistoric stage for the dragons.

Landing on one of the islands of the Komodo national park, we shouldered our filming equipment and hiked into the scorching central highlands. After a while we followed our noses; the stench of a rotting carcass led us to believe that dragons had made a kill nearby. In muddy pools we found mighty water buffalo wallowing, escaping from the overpowering heat. It's difficult to believe that such huge beasts could be felled by a mere lizard. The only dragon we found was huge, fat and happy, and had certainly feasted relatively recently. He was so well-fed that he wouldn't have moved if I'd sat in front of him and given him a big sloppy kiss!

As the sky began to turn gold with the approaching sunset, we trekked into the mountains to find a high viewpoint from which to get our bearings. Once up on top, we had a sublime view over the surrounding islands, but even more exciting was a thoroughly eerie cave entrance, leading to complete darkness. Echoes of whirring bat wings reverberated from the cavern, creating a spooky soundscape that just enticed us in.

This time of year it's pretty hot outside, but inside the cave, it was utterly sweltering. Komodos are known to shelter during the day inside places like this, and as nobody could tell us what lay within, we crept inside with pulses racing. My jungle shirt was soaked with sweat in minutes, and after crawling on my tummy to try to get into some hidden antechambers, was soon covered in bat droppings and mud. Caves are not my favourite places, and the thought that at any second a mighty dragon could lunge out of the darkness made this one even more chilling. In one largish cavern we found a stinking dead deer that had certainly been taken down, and maybe stashed there by a Komodo. Unfortunately, though we scoured the cave, we didn't find a lurking lizard. From the reactions of the crew as we stumbled back out into the fading light, it was obvious they were quite relieved!

To show off the Komodo's killer capabilities we needed to come up with a plan, and to do that we headed to the ranger station on Rinca Island. Komodos are the largest of the varanids, or monitor lizards, so-called because they are said to monitor the presence of crocodiles. Monitors are omnivorous, and will happily scavenge food if they can get it for free.

By the ranger station there was leftover food, as well as extras the dragons could steal, and because of this, around fifteen oversized lizards could always be found. My plan was to string up a chunk of meat in a tree, and watch the dragons tearing it down. I would take a tiny piece of meat on some string and drop it close to the slumbering dragons to lead them the hundred metres or so into the forest towards the main prize. Having spent so much time with these animals, and having seen how lazy they can be, I thought it might take some doing to get their interest. Wrong!

I threw the small chunk of meat towards a group of about eight massive monsters, intending to pull it away and lead them to the meat in the tree. They instantly leapt to their feet and started charging

Filming a Komodo dragon.

towards us. It all happened so quickly that we didn't really have time to react, we just ran. I took the small camera and held it right down in the leading dragon's face as he lumbered towards me, mammoth limbs and clawed feet slapping the ground in a manner that was pure dinosaur. It got great shots, but more than that, meant if the dragon bit anything it would be the camera and not me!

When we got close to the carcass, the dragons' acute sense of taste and smell went into overdrive, but they hadn't located it yet. They just knew there was something tasty around, and went into extreme hunting mode, homing in on the only moving food source. Us!

I'd never seen Komodos like this before. We had big sticks as our only protection, and were honestly having to shove the animals away with all our might, otherwise they would have had a serious go at us. They were canny, one attacking from the front while another doubled back, circling behind us. We were trapped! I was supposed to be watching

Testing the Komodo's bite strength.

the backs of Graham, the cameraman, and Simon, the soundman, as they were busy doing their jobs and couldn't look out for themselves. However, the dragons were coming from all sides. I don't scare easily, but this was a tricky situation. I didn't want to get bitten and I certainly didn't want anything to happen to any of my crew. It seemed far-fetched that the dragons could look on us as food, but it was clear they were hunting us.

Very few people have ever been killed by dragons, but we had just met a ranger who had a horrific scar, where a dragon had nearly taken his leg off . . . the culprit had been around half the size of the lizards surrounding us now.

It was all starting to look bad, when thankfully one of the dragons found the meat. It was as if someone had flicked a switch. The dragons forgot about us in an instant, in favour of the easy source of food. I was able to squat behind the meat in relative safety, as these utterly

prehistoric beasts tore the meat apart, using their entire hefty bodies to rip chunks off it. Why risk injury attacking humans with sticks when you can get free meat for nothing? It told me all I needed to know about how canny these beasts are, while also providing a timely reminder that you NEVER know everything about animals, and that eyes in the back of your head would be a good thing. Maybe I should get wing mirrors fitted to my head . . .

GREEN PIT VIPER (*Trimeresurus albolabris*)

We searched every night on Komodo for this beautiful snake and left without seeing one, but on the island of Bali we found one after just four hours of night searching. They're arboreal and focus on their prey using heat-sensitive pits in the front of the face.

The green pit viper found on Bali.

DRACO LIZARD (*Draco volans*)

An unusual entry on the list, the draco lizard munches bugs in the forest canopy, but when it feels threatened by other predators it launches itself from its perch, spreads its ribs wide and uses the flap of skin between them like a parachute. Apparently dracos can glide as far as sixty metres to another tree or to the ground. This was an animal we weren't planning to feature, but I noticed one trying to look inconspicuous on a tree, and decided we had to try and catch one.

Examining the wing like flaps of skin that allow the draco lizard to glide from tree to tree.

Unfortunately they are almost impossible to get without a net, and we didn't have one! After three hours of leaping up at trees, missing them by a hair's breadth, one of the locals casually reached up, grabbed a draco and passed it to me!

By now we were halfway through filming, and it was starting to get wearing being on the road non-stop. My crew usually stays with me for about three-week stretches, then Johnny and Nick go home, and Graham and Simon come out in their place. I have to be on the road all the time. There's no such thing as a weekend or day off; I seem to be permanently jet-lagged. We follow wildlife rhythms, getting up at dawn, going to bed after a long night-walk and though it is wonderful fun, it can be very tiring. Indonesia though is a little like being home, as it remains one of my favourite places in the world. If all my trips here were put together they would total over a year in the country. I speak the language pretty well and love the place to bits.

Being an archipelago (a chain of islands), Indonesia is incredibly diverse; you can hop from one island to the next, and it's like going to a different country. The people look different and speak a new language. The clan houses, clothing and faces change, and even the landscapes and wildlife can be completely new. Bali and Komodo are close to each other, but they could be on separate continents. My great hero, the naturalist Alfred Russel Wallace, suggested that the reason for this is that there is a deep sea trench lying to the east of Bali, and in ancient times the land masses were actually many kilometres apart. They have never been linked, and the islands to the east are Australasian, while those to the west are Asian.

INLAND TAIPAN (*Oxyuranus microlepidotus*)

There are many snakes that I lust after seeing in the wild, and some that aren't even on my list as it seems so improbable that I will ever see one. Until very recently the inland taipan or fierce snake was one of those. Despite being the most venomous snake, it has never (to our knowledge) killed a human being, as it lives so far from human habitation and has such reclusive habits. However, director Ruth managed to find some special contacts in the far outback of Queensland who thought they might be able to help us. Ruthie, I owe you one…

It was a big journey to get to 'fiercey' country. It took an internal flight, then a drive of many hours to get out into the deep red wilderness. We arrived in prime hunting habitat late in the day, just as the sun was starting to fade, turning the whole landscape a glorious shade of burnished brass. The jeeps pulled up alongside deep red sand dunes, ripples created by outback winds running over the sand like waves. This would make the perfect place for camp. The only time there is any chance of encountering this remarkable snake is shortly after dawn, so we laid our sleeping bags on the ground, cooked our dinner over the open coals of a deadwood fire, and turned in under the stars.

Next morning we were up at 4.00 am when it was still dark, in order to be ready to roll as soon as the sun's rays coursed across the desert. The landscape is a dried up lake bed, dead flat and scorched by

The inland taipan or fierce snake.

temperatures that at midday would be like being in a furnace. Cracks
rent through the dusty ground are the reason this place is home to
the inland taipan. These cracks are occupied by thousands of rodents
and small marsupials which scamper around in underground tunnels,
only coming above the surface after dark. The snakes slither around
in these holes in darkness, occasionally coming face to face with the
teeth of an angry rat or raging bandicoot. They need to strike, inject
their venom and then retreat. Confined spaces could be lethal to the
taipan.

However, if the prey scarpers and runs for even a few minutes it could
be too far gone in the labyrinth of tunnels for our fiercey to find it.
Over time the snake's venom has become more and more potent,
until it is now so intense that the snake can strike, release, then go
and fetch its kill, knowing that the prey animal will have dropped dead
almost instantly.

The reason we were out looking at sunrise is because the road warms up quickly when the sun rises, and the snake comes on to the tarmac in order to soak up some of that energy-giving warmth. They don't want to be out too long; within an hour or so it becomes too hot and they go zipping for cover. We'd come all this way, and really had little more than a couple of hours to find our serpent star.

Reptile spotting was instantly successful. We got a speckled brown and a western brown snake, both more venomous than any snake found in the Americas. We found a sand goanna or monitor lizard, and lots of bearded dragons. It seemed that everything was coming to the road to bask. Soon, however, our hour had expired without any sighting of a fierce snake. Disappointed, we decided to keep driving for a bit. After all, there was a decent wind, which was bringing the temperature down. There was still a chance . . .

An hour and a half later, long after we'd planned to give up our search, I slammed on the brakes. 'Fiercey, fiercy!' yelled Kevin, the local herpetologist (reptile and amphibian specialist), who was sitting next to me. We got out of the car as quickly as possible, and then walked as calmly as we could back towards our hero. The snake was in phenomenal condition, fat from a constant diet of small mammals, and had recently shed its skin, so had a glorious lustre to it. In the winter the snake acquires a jet-black head to complement the golden body with dark edges to each scale. As I got close it drew back its neck into a classic 'S' shape, ready to strike.

For all his extensive experience filming wild animals, this was new for cameraman Gray, and he was at first filming from about ten metres away, not knowing if he'd be safe any closer. On camera you can clearly hear me saying; 'It's OK, Gray, you can get closer than that, it's focused on me,' and it was, eyeing me up suspiciously, ready to strike if I moved too quickly or showed any signs of attacking it.

I lay down behind the serpent superstar, staring into its eyes, knowing that it would be very difficult to ever beat this . . . the most venomous snake on Earth, found in the harshest of outback landscapes. To many people it might just be another snake, but any reptile lover will watch that sequence and know it is something very special indeed.

Getting as close as I dare to an inland taipan.

TOXIC TEST

Inland taipan	0.025
Eastern brown	0.0365
Coastal taipan	0.106
Beaked sea snake	0.1125
Tiger snake	0.131
Saw-scaled viper	0.151
Black mamba	0.32
Spectacled cobra	0.45
Copperhead	0.5
Russell's viper	0.75
King cobra	1.7
Rinkhals	2.65
Mexican rattlesnake	2.8
Adder	6.45
Gaboon viper	12.5
Eastern diamondback	14.6
Lancehead	22
Cottonmouth	25.8
Eyelash viper	33.2
Bushmaster	36.9

This chart refers to the relative toxicity of the venoms of snakes we have featured on Deadly 60, and shows how potent a milligram of toxin is when injected into the skin of a kilo of mice. It should be noted that this has nothing to do with how dangerous these snakes are, or even how potent a bite might be. Just as important is venom yield – how much venom a snake delivers with each bite. For example eastern brown venom is two and half times more toxic than coastal taipan, but the coastal taipan delivers twenty to thirty times more venom in a bite! For anyone who wants to know more, head to Dr Bryan Greig Fry's wonderful website (www.venomdoc.org).

BLUE-RINGED OCTOPUS (*Hapalochlaena* sp.)

The gorgeous blue-ringed octopus is one of the most beautiful animals we have ever featured. You'd be incredibly lucky to actually see one; they're about the size of a golf ball, and rather plain in colour, able to pinch parts of the mantle and the arms to create different shapes, which makes them brilliantly camouflaged. However, if they get angry, excited or feel threatened, they put on a colour show that is truly exquisite. Black-lined, neon-blue circles pulse on a yellow background, warning that this tiny creature should be left well alone. At the centre of the arms is a hard beak that can be coated with a particularly virulent venom. Obviously this is not intended for use against humans, but on at least two well-documented occasions people have picked blue rings up on naked skin, not felt the bite (said to be totally painless) and just hours later dropped dead.

Blue-ringed octopus.

BOX JELLYFISH (*Chironex fleckeri*)

Australia is paradise for a venom hunter like me, and of all the toxic treats to be found here, this is the one that poses most of a threat to us. *The Guinness Book of Animal Records* lists the box jellyfish as being the most venomous animal on Earth, probably because its stinging

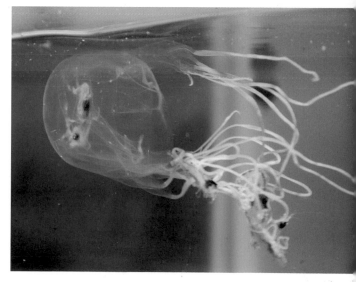

A box jellyfish - the most venomous animal on the planet.

cells can deliver so much venom over such a wide area of their prey (or hapless humans). That's pretty potent considering that the animal is probably ninety-five per cent water. Box jellyfish are found in the seas off the top end of Oz, and grow as the year progresses. When they're at their biggest the seas are totally off limits to swimmers. A single brush with a tentacle can leave a fierce burn that scars for life, many stings could result in the heart simply stopping. Strangely beautiful, but frightening in its potential.

SALTWATER CROCODILE (*Crocodylus porosus*)

The world's largest reptile, with the strongest bite force, is an animal that can trace its lineage back to long before the dinosaurs walked the Earth, and can instil terror and awe in equal measure. My objective was to use our trusty bite force gauge to test out the amount of munch the saltie really can deliver. Old friend and world expert on crocs Adam Britton keeps a big saltwater crocodile in his back garden (really!) for research purposes, and offered to help us. We tied the bite test gauge on to a long bamboo pole and went into his cage. The croc is over five metres long, and Adam calls him Smaug after the dragon in Tolkien's *The Hobbit*. Despite being so enormous, he was totally invisible beneath the aquatic plants, giving us another reminder of what makes these

Saltwater crocodile.

Performing vet checks on Smaug's (much smaller) female mate.

animals so formidable. He was metres in front of me, in quite clear water, yet I couldn't see him at all.

Adam agitated the surface a little to get Smaug's attention, then I splashed the gauge on the surface. The water erupted in jaws, teeth and scales, as Smaug latched on to the stick, chomping down once then retreating. He barely even nudged the gauge itself, but registered an easy 1200 psi! However, this was hardly more than a nibble, so we decided to try again. Perhaps we should have just called it a day . . .

Smaug raged to the surface so quickly he took us all by surprise. He grabbed the gauge and stick in his teeth, and swung his head from side to side. I was still holding on to the pole, and was picked up like a doll and tossed around contemptuously, before being smashed into

Graham, the cameraman, and then into a tree. The strength of the animal was beyond belief. Blood was pouring out of my hand where the pole had sliced into flesh (using bamboo was not a great plan!) and Gray had bruising all down his arm where I'd thundered into him. We waited about an hour before daring to pull the gauge gently out of the water. It was totally destroyed!

Awesome as Smaug was, the most exciting part of our Australian odyssey was still to come. Saltwater crocodiles are now protected here, and are making a real comeback. In some places they are quite a common sight. That's due to the fact that hunting them is now illegal, and also down to captive breeding programmes and monitoring. We were about to get involved with one of the most daring and death-defying of all those programmes. I was joining up with a group who collect croc eggs to raise them in captivity. This can have a massive impact on the survival rate of youngsters. However, the females build their nests in impenetrable reed beds alongside swampy areas of the river. They're just about impossible to get to on foot, but by helicopter it's a different story.

The plan was to fly a chopper over their prime nesting habitat, select a nest, then land on the nearest area of safe dry land. Then we'd hook on to a line slung under the heli, and be lifted up, carried over the marshes and dropped down on top of the nest. Nuts as this sounds, it is what egg collectors do when monitoring the crocodile nests and we did plan our actions very carefully. This was particularly important as the females are extremely protective, and would be right there on the nest guarding it. We'd be going in with local croc wrangler Matt Wright, who is also a hotshot heli pilot. Once we'd located a nest, we were dropped on to an area of grassland, while Matt flew in for a look.

Graham and I stood looking at each other in disbelief, not quite able to compute what we were about to do. Gray just said, 'This is nuts. I mean, you know me, mate, I totally trust you and I'd follow you anywhere, but . . . this is just nuts!'

From a cameraman as talented as Gray, I considered that to be the greatest of compliments, but it was too late to comment, or to change our minds; the chopper was already on its way back to us. The strop beneath the whirlybird dropped down to me and I clipped it into my harness, taking my camera in one hand and a pole and packing crate in the other. These are used to give the female croc something to focus her attention on rather than biting us!

The line tightened, and my feet left the ground. Suddenly the marshes and reed beds were zipping past beneath me, then, there it was! The nest was like a big compost heap and sprawled over the top of it was a three-metre croc, its mouth gaping and looking thoroughly forbidding. The heli plunged me into the

Preparing to board the helicopter.

vegetation alongside Matt, sweat pouring out of every pore in the sweltering humidity. Seconds later Gray dropped in alongside me, his eyes wide open with adrenalin. As soon as Gray was off the line the

Making the descent to the nest.

heli beat a retreat, and suddenly it was silent. We were encased in ceiling-high cane grass, with a croc no more than eight metres away from us. Flies and mosquitoes dabbled around our eyes and noses, probing for moisture, they could have probed anywhere; here we were cut off from the breeze and sweat was gushing out of us.

Matt and I pushed our way through, and soon found why the heli had been necessary – you could never explore this place on foot. We were no more than three metres from the croc before she made her first move, crashing into a pond alongside the nest. We didn't see it, but the noise was like hearing a dragon raging and roaring inside its lair. She was now invisible, but easily within striking range. This was the most frightening and dangerous time.

Gray frantically battled to focus on her, desperately trying to get her on camera. In an instant, she lunged out of the water towards us, jaws wide open, thrashing and bellowing. Poor Gray saw the whole thing in close-up through the viewfinder of his camera, and tumbled straight over on his back in the reeds, thinking she was right on top of him! Matt and I leapt forward brandishing our sticks, prepared to push her away if she went for Gray, but she slipped back into the water and disappeared again. There was no way we could safely look at the nest while she was hiding right alongside it. She had to be driven away, and the only way to do that was to advance.

Matt and I moved towards her and she charged again, so I threw my crate in her direction. She vent her fury on it, crunching it and tossing it about, before deciding enough was enough and thrashing off through the rushes down to the river. We'd bought ourselves a little time, and quickly set to uncovering the eggs. There were about sixty of them, the size and shape of a goose egg, but soft and leathery shelled.

Just about to land next to the nest with a crate for the eggs.

Matt collected them incredibly carefully, protecting the developing baby croc inside despite his shaking hands and the sweat pouring from his face.

Just five minutes later we were done, and Matt called in the chopper to haul us out. We'd completed a small piece of the puzzle that will hopefully lead to the continued survival of this magnificent beast. Throughout most of its former range around the world salties are persecuted and face localised extinction. If more places can learn the wonder of the croc as they have here in Oz, the future of the saltwater croc will finally be secured.

TASMANIAN DEVIL (*Sarcophilus harrisii*)

These animals are the marsupial equivalent of a mustelid (see page 49) with an attitude to match. They're mostly scavengers, but will sometimes take live prey. Looking at them, they seem totally out of proportion, with an enormous head, round body and tiny little legs. The reason the head is so oversized is down to the massive bony skull, and the mammoth muscles that drive the jaw. Being close to one as

Filming Tasmanian devils.

it feeds sets your teeth on edge, hearing them grinding and crunching through bone and sinew! However, it's their attitude that gives them their bad reputation. They have the capacity to turn into a howling, screeching, whirling dervish, lashing out at everything around them; particularly other devils. This is how they got their name – early settlers heard them wailing in the forests and assumed there were real devils living there!

COPPERHEAD (*Austrelaps superbus*)

Australia was always going to be big on snakes, so I had to fight for a chance to search for them again while we were in Tasmania. Luckily though, our attempt to film platypus didn't succeed, which gave me greater leverage to insist on a day's snake hunting. The first thing that happened as we trekked through marshy coastal meadows, was that

Searching for snakes in Tasmania.

Graham came within a finger's breadth of stepping on one of the most venomous snakes in the world. The tiger snake was massive, and we were to find seven of them that afternoon, but we've featured them on Deadly before, so ideally I wanted to find something different . . . another Tazzie classic that loves these swampy habitats for the same reason as the tigers; there's oodles of frogs here for them to feed on.

I'd never found this particular species before, so when we finally saw one my heart leapt. It was a copperhead, glossy black above and deep burnished scarlet beneath, as thick as my arm, which is verging on obese for a snake of this length. It was so big 'cos it'd been feasting on endless amounts of frogs, using a venom that is probably more toxic than any snake outside Australia. It was strangely beautiful, and very much worthy of a place on the Deadly 60 list.

Taking a look at a copperhead.

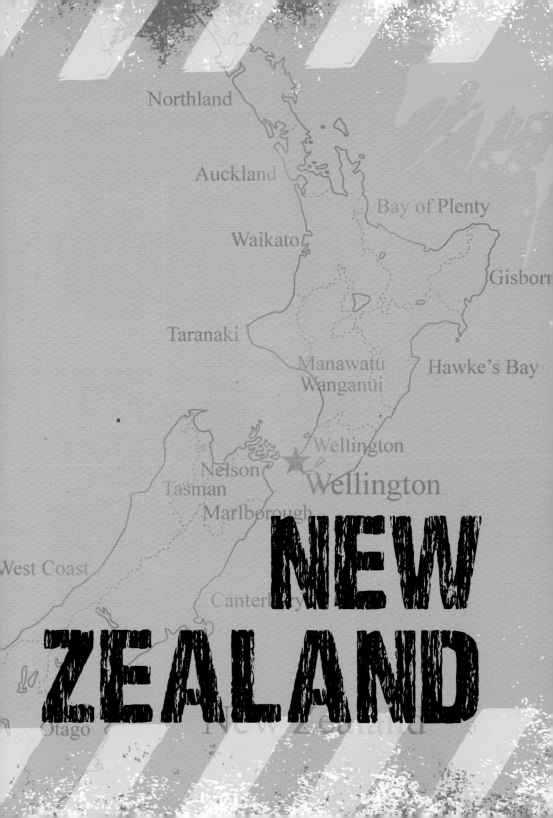

KEA (*Nestor notabilis*)

Now we've had some tenuous animals on Deadly 60 over the years, but a parrot? Surely that is the least convincing candidate ever? Well, actually the kea is a remarkable bird, and with several really rather deadly attributes. First of all they're alpine birds, living in the often freezing environment of the New Zealand mountains. Secondly,

Filming a kea.

they're incredibly intelligent, always thieving stuff and experimenting with things in their world to see if they might be good to eat. Thirdly, they are on occasion fairly vicious predators. They've been seen raiding other birds' nests to take their chicks, killing rabbits, and have even been seen attacking sheep, ripping the fat and eyes out of live animals!

SPERM WHALE (Physeter macrocephalus)

We have some real animal record-breakers on Series Three of Deadly, but the sperm whale must be one of the most dramatic. They're the owners of the largest brain of any animal, the largest toothed animal, and the deepest diving animal known. Most of their dives reach one thousand metres and some dives are certainly much much deeper.

Sperm whales battle with giant squid in the infinite darkness above the abyssal plains of the deep ocean, and they are mythical, magical beasts. They are named for the milky, waxy substance found inside their heads called spermaceti. This material is probably partially for buoyancy, and also acts as a medium for concentrating the world's most potent natural sonar (another record). The sonic clicks of the sperm whale are created by an organ known as the phonic lips, then transmitted out through the spermaceti organ. They bounce back off the environment and their prey, and are received in the lower jaw, giving the whale an accurate picture of what's around them. We intended to use sonar to find a sperm whale, but more of that later.

We decided to scan the seas of the coastal town of Kaikoura in a helicopter, to see if we could locate a sperm whale from the air. It's always exciting going up in a chopper with the door open, seeing the world racing past, sun glinting off the sea, wind rushing past your face. Our pilot took us straight out to sea, heading for the area where sperm whales are known to come closest to land. The reason why Kaikoura is

Preparing to take to the skies in search of sperm whales.

one of the best places in the world to see sperm whales is its undersea topography. Not more than a few kilometres from shore is a deep sea trench, with waters many thousands of metres deep. Sperm whales love to hunt in these waters, chasing the abundant squid, and it wasn't long before we saw one. There was a mere puff of what looked like steam in the distance, which was in fact the mist from its blowhole. At first I was disappointed, as there was a whale-watching boat right alongside our prize, which seemed to spoil it, as the whale wasn't ours and ours alone. However, the boat gave us a sense of scale. As we hovered above, and Graham the cameraman filmed our prize below, we could quite easily see that it was as long as the whale-watching boat, which must have been near twenty metres long. It's usually the fully grown males that reach that length. It was an exciting taste of what was to come.

The following day, we headed out in a boat to try and encounter a sperm whale in its own watery world. Instantly the seas around us came alive. We had perhaps eight different species of albatross approaching the boat, including the biggest of them all, the wandering albatross; the bird with the largest wingspan on Earth, perhaps over four metres! There were seals, dolphins, and vast numbers of seabirds, all of them obviously tied to the Kaikoura coast by the wealth of seafood beneath the waves.

Finding a sperm whale would be tricky, but once we saw one at the surface we should certainly be able to get a shot if we could get close enough. Their behaviour is quite predictable; they dive for around an hour, then surface and breathe deeply, ridding themselves of toxic carbon dioxide, and getting precious oxygen into their blood. They stay in almost the same spot, barely moving, for eight to nine minutes, before diving again with a single mighty lash of their tail flukes.

In order to pinpoint the whales while they were still underwater, we had a hydrophone. This highly directional waterproof mic picks up the sounds that the sperm whale makes as it's hunting. After a few hours at sea being tossed around fairly frantically by the waves, we zoned in on a whale. We saw it at a distance, lying close to a whale-watching boat, but by the time we were close it had already decided to dive. This pattern continued throughout the day. Tracking them by their sounds, though, was thrilling. Down deep and hunting, the piercing clicks of their echolocation were almost constant. Then about fifty-five minutes after they'd gone under, everything would go silent, as they were heading to the surface. From there on in, everyone was on high alert, binoculars focused on the sea around us.

One of the things that really counts in my favour when it comes to wildlife watching is that I don't get seasick – so far! We spend so much time at sea on very small boats, tossed about by waves, and members of the crew who do get ill have the worst time of their lives. For me, once I get into the zone of watching for wildlife I plain forget about the pitch and toss of the boat, but even so, nine hours at sea under burning sun, wind and spray on a small boat starts to chip away at your resolve.

Finally, at around 5.00 pm a whale surfaced nearby. The relief on board was enormous, but not as enormous as the whale. It was so huge it was just totally mesmerising. These whales have been known to reach sixty tonnes . . . about the same as six ten-tonne trucks, or a small passenger plane. As soon as we were close, I unstrapped the inflatable kayak from the deck and slipped overboard. Normally boats have to stay fifty metres away from the whales, but we had special permission to approach – just once – in the kayak, in order to film. I paddled gently, not wanting to spook the whale during the important time that he was resting and getting ready for his next dive. When I was just metres away, he drove air and water vapour out through his blowhole, and it saturated me. It smelt somewhat stale and rather fishy!

It wasn't really until my kayak pulled up alongside the whale that I had any sense of quite how big he actually was. I was totally and utterly dwarfed by this marine monster. A deep sense of awe flooded through me in the presence of this giant, an animal of regal majesty. Running down his head I could see deep white scars caused by the

raking of other sperm whale teeth while in combat. I didn't see the sucker marks of giant squid, but scientists have used such scars to determine that there are squid in the oceans even larger than the ones we know about. These creatures have been washed up on beaches, and have been up to eighteen metres long, with eyes the size of dustbin lids. The struggles between such squid and sperm whales must be the most titanic on Earth.

Too soon the whale puffed out one last time, and with a sweep of his mighty tail moved forward. Then he ducked his head and his tail went up into the air, towering high above me, water pouring off the flukes and reflecting in the sun. It was so overwhelming, I felt that there should have been loud, massive splashes and thunderous whale-song, but no, it was totally silent. And, in an instant the animal was a mere memory. All that remained was a tranquil patch of water where he'd been, and a lone fur seal playing oblivious in the middle of it. Wow!

WHALING NOT YET DEAD

These mighty mammals have long been hunted for their meat, fat and other properties, and in the heyday of whaling hundreds of thousands were taken from the seas every year. Sperm whales, with their habit of being still at the surface for long periods of time were easy targets for whalers with explosive harpoons and tracking equipment. In time, people realised that this hunting was not sustainable and the International Whaling Commission voted for a ban on whaling. Whales are huge animals and their populations take a long time to regenerate. If hunted extensively, their numbers crash and may never recover, yet some nations still continue whaling even today.

GLOW-WORM (*Arachnocampa luminosa*)

In certain cave systems, the larvae of the fungus gnat hunt flying insects using a cunning trick. The larvae drop down mucous threads coated with sticky goo. The gnats then start glowing, using a combination of different chemicals and enzymes to create a greeny light that is remarkably efficient as it's made almost without residual heat. The light attracts flying insects like mayflies and mosquitoes, which become entangled and are drawn towards the mouth of the gnat larvae. It's all rather grotesque, but eerily beautiful at the same time.

Getting ready to abseil into the Waitomo Caves in search of glow-worms.

SAILFISH (*Istiophorus albicans*)

One of the fastest fish in the sea, sailfish are also known to be one of the most difficult to find and film. They're what's known as a 'pelagic', that is deep-sea species, and stick to the open ocean, far from shore and never in the same place twice. In order to find them, we had to enlist the help of other animals in their world, predominantly birds.

Sailfish are aquatic assassins, zooming in at up to 109 km/h on other fish. In response to the presence of speedsters, smaller fish come together in protective formations known as baitballs. Such a bonanza of food attracts frigate birds from above. We kept our eyes on the horizon for the frigate birds, and if we saw them flocking at the surface, we'd have to get in quick-smart to stand a chance of filming the sailfish hunting beneath.

Sailfish are not only difficult to find, but really hard to film too. We'd spent two days trying in Mozambique in Africa and saw nothing at all. As they move so fast, we'd have to power up close in the boat then leap overboard and swim like crazy. There'd be no time to kit up in scuba gear – we'd have to do it all free-diving, with only the air in our lungs. Underwater cameraman Simon and I would also power along after them with whacking great waterproof cameras in tow; Simon's weighed as much as two sacks of potatoes. All in all, it was a mighty gamble, but if it came off, it'd be one of Deadly's greatest ever achievements.

We set out to sea a little after dawn. Conditions were good and clear, waves were a bit bumpy, but the visibility looked superb. All we needed was some very big, very fast fish. After the initial excitement, it turned into a long, humdrum day, plodding back and forth across the sea, seeing nothing. After a full day of being hammered by weather, sun and wind, we were all feeling pretty frazzled and seasick, and were beginning to suspect this had been a gamble too far.

We were genuinely just about to turn for shore, late into the afternoon after eight hours of being tossed about by the waves, when on the horizon I spotted what looked like a swarm of bees. 'Errr . . . guys . . . it's err . . . frigate birds . . . there, look!'

If I had doubted myself for a second, the reactions of the boat crew soon put that to rest. They leapt up as if electrocuted, and put the boat into warp speed as we shot towards the flock of birds, Simon and I trying to get our gear on while being flung all over the place by the bouncing boat. When we got close, it was clear we had something very special. The dorsal fins of the sailfish were clearly visible, slicing

Sailfish.

through the waves like little sharks, and the frigate birds were raking the surface with their beaks, trying to snatch a sardine snack.

Simon and I dropped in four times before we even managed to get a glimpse of the action. It was all moving so quickly that it shot away from us long before we could get to

Sailfish hunting sardines.

it. Each time we held off from dropping in just a few seconds longer, hoping to get closer and closer to the baitball. Finally, we slipped overboard right on top of it. I have never seen anything so spectacular. There were maybe forty sailfish, each of them longer than I am tall and perhaps around my weight.

That was where all comparisons ended. They zipped through the water at speeds that seemed impossible, dorsal fins folded flat against their bodies, long spear-like bills lashing out at the shimmering baitball in front of them. They used their bills to separate sardines, before snapping them down in a gulp, and moving on to the next. The silvery sardines were swerving this way and that to try to escape, but their end was a foregone conclusion.

We dropped in on them again and again, finning for all we were worth. With my smaller, lighter camera I was able to get ahead of Simon into the action, and for the first (and only) time I was getting better shots than the master himself! At one point, I found myself right in among the baitball, and totally alone. Simon had been left behind and the sardines decided to take shelter behind the only cover available: me! For one horrid moment it looked as if I'd surely be skewered. Bills were lashing perilously close to my face and my legs. One big sailfish swam right between my legs. It was utter carnage!

Diving with sailfish.

It was, however, too spectacular to be frightening. We had nearly an hour in the water with the sailfish before they finally decimated the baitball. As the dark hunters disappeared off into the big blue, all that was left behind in the water was shimmering scales. They drifted down through the water like snowflakes, the only trace of the annihilated sardines. What more fitting way to mark the halfway point of filming – thirty animals – than with the fastest fish in the seas nearly turning me into a giant shish kebab!

BULL SHARK (*Carcharhinus leucas*)

The aptly named bull shark is a thuggish-looking shark, stocky and blunt-nosed. They look like trouble. They're truly adaptable sharks, capable of travelling thousands of kilometres inland into freshwater

Bull shark.

ecosystems, and hunting in the murkiest estuaries using acute senses of smell and electroreception and sensitivity to vibration. They take a terrific variety of prey, from small fish and crustaceans to turtles, other sharks, even mammals. They have a reputation for being maneaters, and are confirmed as having killed people in the past, but this is fantastically rare. Just quite how little danger they pose to humans can be shown by the fact that we went diving with them right alongside one of the world's busiest tourist beaches!

Filming in
underwater caves.

MEXICAN NIGHT SNAKE (*Elaphe flavirufa*)

Deep in a cave system filled with bats lurks one of the most dazzling snake spectacles on Earth. Local people call this the 'cave of the hanging serpents', and no wonder. There is a small but extremely healthy population of snakes living inside that have learned how to feast on flying bats as they head out to feed. The team and I had visualised hundreds of snakes dangling down at the entrance to the cave . . . well, that was perhaps a little naive. Instead we spent a good couple of hours scouring the visible parts of the cave, and only found one. When we sat down puzzled, our guide quietly commented that this had been a waste of time, as the snakes only emerged at dusk when the bats start to fly out to feed. Oops.

I find a Mexican night snake..

We exited the cave, and sat in the forest being munched by mosquitoes for a few hours, waiting for dusk to fall. Finally the light faded, and the first few bats started fluttering through the trees. The whole team went down into the cave, but then just soundie Nick, cameraman Johnny and I climbed into a smaller chamber higher up the cave wall, and crawled in on our hands and knees. There was a snake; its head dangling down into the air while its tail was anchored to the rock. The second our lights fell on him though the snake swiftly

withdrew into the cracks. We had been warned this might happen. Clearly conventional filming was not going to work here.

Our next tactic was to go in under a light they would not be able to see; infrared. Unfortunately, humans can't see in it either. I said goodbye to the crew, and crawled off under the knee-high ceiling into total darkness with no torch, seeing solely through the tiny screen on the infrared camera. It was beyond spooky. Bats in their thousands were pelting past my ears, brushing my face with their wings. Unseen cockroaches and venomous centipedes scuttled over my hands as I blundered on in the black, feeling my way with my fingertips. Ancient bat dung was crammed under my fingernails and smeared all over my clothes and face, the ammonia stench searing my nostrils. It was all pretty unpleasant!

Finally I found a couple of perfect bottlenecks, where the bats were being funnelled through on their way out to hunt. As expected, each exit had its own resident snake, hanging down snatching at bats as they passed. I sat hunched under the rock roof, focused on one for nearly an hour, until finally he seemed to lose interest and wriggled up into his hole. The other snake was about twenty metres away, but it took me about five minutes to get there on my hands and knees, grovelling through the dirt and unable to see anything. As soon as I was in position and managed to get my snake in the viewfinder it struck. NO! It'd caught a bat, but I'd missed the shot by a millisecond.

I crawled closer, knowing that while it was occupied with trying to kill the bat it wouldn't be concerned about me. The snake wrapped several curls of its body around the bat and started to crush. The bat was shaking, trying to get free, but the snake's wickedly pointed teeth were deep in its fur, and the air was already being squeezed out of its lungs. It was no more than a minute before the bat was dead and the snake uncurled, and started to manoeuvre it into position to swallow it. Scientists have shown that constricting snakes can sense the heartbeat of a prey animal, and when they feel it has stopped, they'll stop constricting, not wanting to use any more energy than is necessary to kill.

Exasperated that I'd failed to get the killer shot, we came back the next night, and again I spent five hours crawling around in the bat guano alone and in pitch darkness, shuttling backwards and forwards between my two snakes, who were in exactly the same position as the previous night. It was easily the most awkward filming job I've ever attempted, but there was simply no other way of doing it. The second a hunting snake sensed my presence, it would simply slip away, and not re-emerge for as much as half an hour.

One of them made three kills that night, but I was never quite there in time to film it. In my defence, I was trying to move silently through

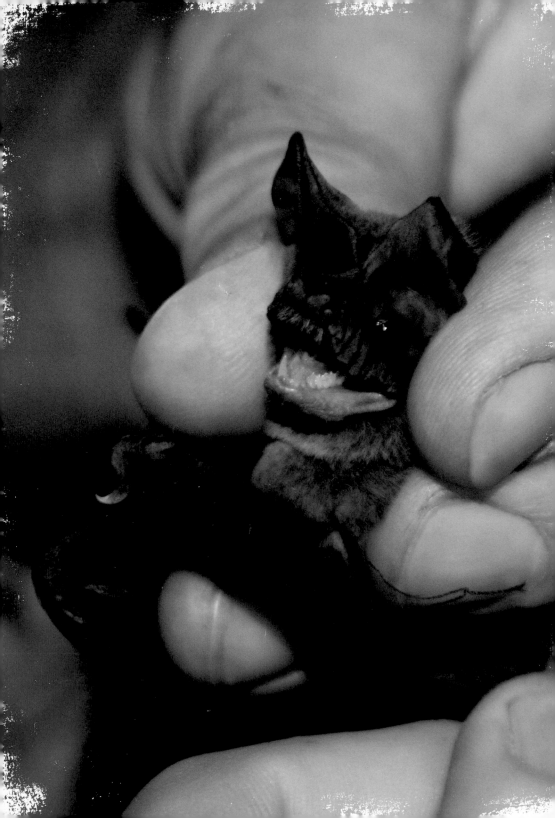

the cave with one hand full of infrared torch, the other full of camera, totally blind and up to my wrists in dung – it was a miracle I got anything at all! Finally though, when I'd decided we could get no more under infrared light, I waited till one of the snakes had made a kill and called Johnny in. Under normal white light, he got some breathtaking shots of the snake scoffing a bat right in front of my face. Truly memorable stuff.

BAT VOLCANO

We took the unusual step of putting all the species of bats from the bat volcano on our list. We travelled to a sinkhole dropping straight down into the limestone rock of the Yucatan peninsula. Come dusk, the sinkhole started to reverberate with the squeaks of vocalising bats, and the whirr of their wings, amplified by the loudspeaker of the rocky bowl. Then they funnelled out over the forests in great smoky trails, hundreds of thousands of bats off to eat tonnes of flying insects in that night alone. Each bat might eat half its own body weight in insects. In terms of scale, it was the greatest display of predation we had ever filmed on Deadly 60.

MORELET'S CROCODILE

(*Crocodylus moreletii*)
There have been many species of croc in this series, but this one

Meeting a Morelet's crocodile.

probably vies with the gharial and the Orinoco for the title of most endangered. Morelet's croc is almost only found along the east coast of Mexico, and is not one of the largest species, rarely growing over three metres in length.

The crocs do, however, have one thing that very much counts against them. Whereas many species have tough scaly skin with dermal bones (bony plates inside the skin), and therefore are of limited use for leather, the Morelet's has glorious silky skin with beautiful patterning. Somewhat inevitably they have been hunted to the very brink of extinction. We were lucky enough to be out searching for them with the conservation biologists who have been responsible for bringing them back. We spotlighted for crocs for two nights, but never got close enough to catch one, until finally we picked out the eyeshine of a decent-sized animal in among the lilies on a clear-water lake.

We pursued the beast in our boat for about ten minutes or so, the croc swimming fast underwater to evade us. While they can remain submerged for many hours if they're still and not burning energy and oxygen, if they are working hard they have to surface much more regularly. Finally it came up, and I slipped a noose over its head and drew it up on board. The scientists ran a slew of tests on the beautiful animal as I cradled it in my arms, as close to pretty as a croc could ever be!

GREEN MORAY EEL (*Gymnothorax funebris*)

The green moray is the largest of the moray eels. It has four nostrils, the better to scent its prey, and will actively hunt over a reef by night, or hide in a crevice waiting for unwary prey to swim nearby.

I find a young Morelet's crocodile.

GIANT SCOLOPENDRA (*Scolopendra gigantea*)

People often ask me if there are any animals I'm scared of, and I always say no. However, if I'm honest, big centipedes do give me the creeps. It's not exactly an irrational fear; some of them are easily venomous enough to kill a person, and those that aren't could put you in terrible agonising pain for hours or even days. However it's not that,

A giant scolopendra, the largest centipede on the planet.

it's something about the way they move that really gets me. A big centipede is harder to handle than any snake, and in Venezuela I was about to tangle with the biggest on Earth.

I first learned of its existence when watching David Attenborough's *Life in the Undergrowth*. This centipede was as long as my forearm and climbed up into the roof of a cave to catch bats on the wing. Not only was it grotesque, it was also fascinating; an invertebrate with a miniscule brain, yet with the forethought and strategy to cross metres of empty rock, take up position and ambush flying bats. It was called the giant scolopendra.

Every time a good natural history story comes my way, I get on the phone and try to find out how we can film it. With the centipede this proved tricky. The bat catching was only known in one cave system in Venezuela, and that had just been ravaged by fire. Perhaps our chance had passed. But then, as we were putting the finishing touches to the schedule for Series Three, word reached us of another cave where the monstrous centipedes had been spotted – we were on!

Venezuela is one of my top locations to film wildlife, but working there wasn't easy. Just getting to the location was dangerous as we had to travel through major cities and they, like all cities around the world, have their problems. Simply put, chasing the most venomous invertebrates on Earth was the least of our worries!

Reaching our location was a full-on mission. We had a flight, then half a day's driving, then about an hour off-road even to get to the trailhead that led to the cave. We'd been hoping to get even closer in the jeep, so we could take all our fancy filming equipment and climbing stuff right to the cave itself. However, torrential rains had turned the paths into a quagmire. The jeep was a massive 4x4, so our driver, Jesus, drove hard at a muddy slope trying to get up it. The mud was waist high, and he promptly got stuck. The only way to get him out was by attaching the winch to a tree and revving the thing up. Mud flew everywhere, covering us all, and eventually we got it out, but we gave up on driving, and decided to trudge the last hour or so.

When we got there, the cave was truly eerie, and a fitting home for a macabre creepy-crawly. The place stank, and because there were fungal spores in the air we had to wear face masks, so we didn't catch a lethal disease called histoplasmosis. Inside, the floor was laden with centuries of bat droppings, which were alive with cockroaches, whip spiders and scorpions. In one corner I found some black tarry mess that was clearly the droppings of vampire bats. Using my butterfly net I managed to catch one of these Deadly favourites, and get a glance at possibly the sharpest teeth on Earth . . . hard to believe these snappy bats could actually become food . . . for a centipede!

Only a few weeks before I'd filmed snakes catching bats in Mexico (see page 132) and noticed that they wouldn't do anything while there was white light around. Having learned my lesson, I instructed the team to turn off all their lights, and trusty cameraman Graham and I wandered around with infrared cameras, checking every dark corner and crevice for signs of our monster. No luck. After about eight hot, humid, stinking hours in the revolting cave we were all thoroughly creeped out, exhausted and ready for the long drive back to town and our hotel.

The following day we returned in low spirits. Nobody wanted to go back into that horrid place. It felt like somewhere that people were not welcome, a kind of black hell, full of sinister animals that meant us harm. As we were walking down to the cave a local family whose house was close to the trail called us in. They had found something interesting in their vegetable patch. We went in with the cameras rolling, not really expecting anything special, and the man of the house handed me an ice bucket. I took the lid off to reveal the biggest centipede I have ever seen.

This species can exceed thirty centimetres in length. If you can't visualise that, it's the length of a standard ruler, or the distance from my elbow to my knuckles. This one was nearly that long, as thick as a baby's wrist and a rich scarlet colour. My first thought was to take it out wearing sturdy gardening gloves, and let it run free over them. It instantly became clear that this was a terrible idea. It was so quick that there was no way I'd be able to manoeuvre it safely. At the head end, the front two legs have become modified into venom-injecting claws called forcipules. On this particular specimen, they were long, curved, needle-sharp and powerful enough to cheerfully bite straight through the thinner material on the back of my fingers and hands. That would have been all bad.

I gripped the centipede for dear life, but it was the strongest animal for its size that I have ever handled. Invertebrates can be disproportionately strong

Giant scolopendras need careful handling.

thanks to the way their muscles connect to their solid exoskeleton – their hard outer structure. This formidable beast squeezed itself through my fingers no matter how hard I clasped it. With the cameras still rolling, I talked about it for a few minutes, the entire time focused on the writhing monster in my hands. When I finally put it back in the box, I realised that the crew hadn't said a word the whole time. They were all looking at me, shell-shocked. Laura, the director, gave me a big hug and looked as if she was about to burst into tears.

'I've never been so happy to see an animal go back into a box,' she said. 'I was sure you were going to get bitten.'

It was very tempting after that triumph not to go back into the Cave of Doom, but our mood had been so buoyed by our experience that we decided to give it a go, if only for a few hours. It was a good decision. Simon, the smiley sound recordist, spotted a black scolopendra near the entrance, and though it wasn't as big or frightening as the first centipede, finding it inside the cave was a much nicer sequence. Well, I say nicer. Actually it was thoroughly chilling. Scuttly, sinister, seriously venomous . . . scolopendra.

Filming Orinoco crocodiles.

ORINOCO CROCODILE

(*Crocodylus intermedius*)
The scientific name *intermedius* refers to the fact that the snout of an Orinoco croc is quite slender; between that of the crazy thin gharial and other crocodilians. They're highly endangered, and would probably be

extinct without human intervention. I worked together with a local crocodile conservation project to take the eggs from an Orinoco croc nest, so they could be raised in captivity. This removes the pressure from scavengers and predators, and radically increases the ratio of hatchlings that will make it to a year in age.

GREEN ANACONDA (*Eunectes murinus*)

The green anaconda is the world's largest, heaviest, strongest snake. Females bear live young, and need enormous amounts of bulk and fat reserves to enable them to provide valuable calories for the unborn babies. They can reach nearly nine metres in length, though in actual fact anacondas of over five metres are extremely unusual. In order to find anacondas, you have to wade through the pools around the flooded Llanos, preferably barefoot and feeling

The green anaconda – heaviest of all snakes.

for the presence of anacondas with your toes. If you step on something hard it's a croc, if it's soft and leathery it's a big snake! This may sound risky, but most of the crocodiles are spectacled caiman, which will usually beat a hasty retreat when they sense you coming.

ELECTRIC EEL (*Electrophorus electricus*)

Electric eels are animals I have a huge amount of respect for, and with good reason. Four years previously, on an expedition in Guyana, I was trying to catch a big crocodile at night, aiming to tempt it close to shore by slapping the water with a fish. Suddenly I was blown clear off my feet, and landed flat on my back two metres from the water! I knew instantly what had happened, and ran back up to camp to get Johnny the cameraman. By the time we came back, a huge, fat electric eel was up on the bank looking for the prey animal it had shocked! It was about a metre and a half long and as fat as my calf, with an orange underside. Thoroughly creepy. What was worse was that when I chatted to our ichthyologist (fish scientist) about it, he told me I'd had a very lucky escape; if I'd been in the water I would probably have been killed.

An electric eel.

So it was with some trepidation that the crew and I pulled up at a choice location in Venezuela to film electric eels. It was the dead of night, but still humid, the air thick with moths and mosquitoes bumping around in our head-torch light. In natural environments, the eels group in deep pools below waterfalls, hunting fish as they gather to move upstream. Here on a working cattle ranch, the space below a dam served the same purpose. As we parked on a bridge over the water, we could see the mysterious shapes of dozens of eels coming to the surface to breathe. Electric eels often live in murky waters where the oxygen content is low, and can gulp air to supplement the oxygen they take in through their gills.

Now obviously I wasn't going to just wander into the brown murky water dressed normally. Instead I donned rubber overalls to insulate myself from potential shocks. The night was so sticky and close that it felt as if we were breathing warm treacle; dressing in rubber from head to toe didn't help me cool down! The overalls wouldn't protect me against all of the river residents either – the water was stacked

In search of electric eels.

full of crocodiles, literally hundreds of them. I had to shoo them out of the way to get into the water. There was a lump in my throat as I waded into the dark, water up to my chest. The pool had zero visibility and was certainly filled with things that could easily kill me. I couldn't blame anyone else; it was my idea to catch an eel, because I'd seen how many there were in the pool, and I'd thought it would be a piece of cake. Surely I'd only be in the water for ten or fifteen minutes? It would all be too easy . . .

But this was uncharted territory. None of the locals were dumb enough to wade out into eel and croc-infested waters at night, so we had no knowledge of how difficult it would be. Perhaps if I'd read a bit more carefully about the eels before, I'd have realised that they use their electrical powers a bit like radar, and are highly sensitive to anything new in their environment. Beforehand they'd been regularly surfacing close to the bridge, but as soon as I was in, the eels stayed in deeper water.

I waited with my net for nearly five hours. Every so often a grotesque pink and brown monster would pop up close by and I'd swipe with the net, but they'd slip out of it at the last minute. Crocs would surface nearby, making me want to squeal with fear, and despite coming ever so close to catching an eel once or twice, it was what is nowadays known as an 'epic fail'. Exhausted, and with nerves frayed from having fear-adrenalin zipping round my body for so long, we retired to bed, vowing to return the following night.

Next evening we came back, and I waded out again, this time with much less light, and moving impossibly slowly and carefully. When I reached the deepest spot I could stand in without water slopping over the top of my waders, I agitated the surface with my hand, in a way I hoped would replicate the thrashing of a struggling fish. The eels came straight over to check it out. However, they'd pop up right alongside me with no warning, and I didn't want to make a stab with the net, as any undue commotion would have spooked them and ruined things. Twice I got an eel partially into the net, only for it to slip out again. Every time, the crew up on the bridge above would cheer then groan as the eel escaped. Turns out, eels really are as slippery as . . . well, as an eel.

By midnight, my nerves were shot to bits, but I was determined not to give up. There was no way I was being beaten by a fish – even if it is the most powerful electricity-producing animal on Earth. I stood motionless, willing a particularly big eel to come closer. Finally, he was just a metre in front of me, and I dipped the net to the bottom, and ever so slowly raised it to the surface. When it was clear that he was mostly inside, I whipped it up as fast as possible . . . success! He was a huge eel, perhaps eight kilos in weight and as long as my leg. The crowd gathered up on the bridge went crazy, as if I'd just scored a goal for Venezuela against Brazil! Wading back past the crocodiles, I felt like a hero. However, there was one more twist to the tale.

We put the eel into a big white cooler box, with two electrodes attached to a speaker in the water. You could hear loud clicking as the

Getting ready to test the eel.

animal generated charge from the organs that occupy about two thirds of its body, functioning like organic batteries. Whenever it moved, the clicks increased in volume and frequency. Even just slithering gently in the tub it generated in excess of 110 volts. When shocking prey, eels have been known to hit 600 volts; easily enough to stop a human heart. Given confidence by my hours and hours in the water, protected

Ouch!

by my rubber waders and gloves, I put both hands in at once to pick up the eel and show it to the camera. Maybe it was the dampness of my sweat, perhaps small holes in the rubber gloves. Whatever, I unexpectedly connected the circuit. It was as if I had grabbed an electric cow fence. I jumped backwards, very nearly swearing, before the whole crew dissolved into giggles. Seriously though, if I had got that kind of shock from an eel at rest and wearing all that protective clothing, imagine what it could do at full blast. It doesn't bear thinking about . . .

BRAZIL

February 2012

BLACK PIRANHA (*Serrasalmus rhombeus*)

There are more than thirty species of piranha, some of which feed only on fruit that's fallen into the water. That is certainly not the case with the giant black piranha. This is the biggest of the group, I've seen them at perhaps forty centimetres in length, and they get a bit bigger than that. As youngsters they sneakily nip off the fins and chunks of the tails of other fish, but when they get bigger they savage much larger prey.

Heading up the
Amazon in search
of black piranha.

A black
piranha. Look at
those teeth.

WOLF FISH (*Hoplias malabaricus*)

These toothy, slippery beasts can reach up to a metre in length, and stalk the dark rivers of the Amazon basin at dusk, in search of other fish to feed on.

We find some wolf fish and get a chance to examine the deadly teeth.

MANED WOLF (*Chrysocyon brachyurus*)

A rare opportunity to see a maned wolf.

Looking rather like a fox that's had its legs and ears stretched, the maned wolf is something of a canine animal oddity. They stalk the savannahs of South America, using those long legs to get up high above the grasses and spot rodent prey. Unusually though, they are one of the most frugivorous (fruit feeding) of all the dog family, and will spend a good deal of their day trotting round woodlands in search of fallen fruit.

JAGUAR

(*Panthera onca*)

The only animal we've tried to find on all three series of Deadly . . . and failed. I'm not giving up yet though, as this is, pound for pound, probably the most powerful of all big cats. Its jaw is so strong that

it delivers a killing bite clear through the head of its prey; even thick-skulled beasts like wild pigs.

Searching for jaguar tracks, but no success.

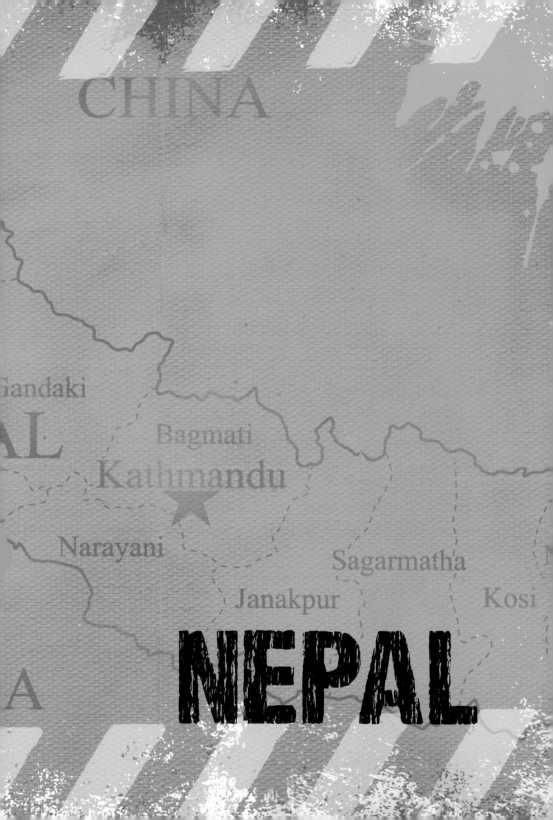

TIGER (*Panthera tigris*)

The Bengal tiger is an old Deadly favourite, the largest cat on Earth and a fearsome feline capable of feasting on prey as large as water buffalo. We tracked them over several days of driving Nepalese trails and using camera traps, and finally saw one strolling down a track in the golden light of dusk. Unfortunately a blazing forest fire started moving towards us, and we had to evacuate the area but still had the privilege of being in the presence of true animal royalty.

EGYPTIAN VULTURE (*Neophron percnopterus*)

Vultures have a pretty lousy reputation. Most species have slightly grotty naked heads to prevent their feathers being sullied when they plunge their heads into a rotting carcass. They have terrible table manners, and New World vultures poo and wee down their legs to keep themselves cool. There is no doubt though that they are vital to the health of wild ecosystems, and in flight are truly impressive.

One species that probably inspires less revulsion than others is the beautiful Egyptian vulture. Their white plumage with black and grey trim makes them rather handsome birds, and they have the unique skill of being able to break into eggs as tough as ostrich eggs by gently tapping them open with stones, making sure not to split the shell and tip the contents into the dust. This makes them one of the few tool-wielding birds. First we went to a location in

the lowlands where vultures were quite commonplace and set ourselves up in a hide. About eighty metres in front of the hide we ditched the carcass of a recently deceased cow. Now all we had to do was sit back and wait. Unfortunately, I've attempted this with vultures many times, and they are always more reticent than one might imagine. On one memorable trip in the Caucasus Mountains of Central Asia, we staked out a carcass for three days. Vultures circled above us, watching very carefully, but were clearly too clever to descend while we were watching them. On the third day, we decided to take an hour-long break away from the hide. When we came back, the carcass was gone.

I meet Kevin, a rescued, rehabilitated Egyptian vulture.

This time around it looked as though things could go the same way. We sat there for three hours and the vultures landed in nearby trees, watching us, watching the dead cow, but doing nothing at all. We were running out of time before we would have to drive up into the mountains, and couldn't wait all day. Just as we'd decided to give up, the first bird dropped down to the cow and wandered over to it. It was as if someone had rung the dinner bell. Literally hundreds of vultures from eight different species dropped from the trees and the skies and buried themselves up to their necks in the meat. Feathers flew, and dung, blood and dust scattered everywhere in a true feeding frenzy. Thirty minutes later the vultures were gone, and so was every scrap of meat. All that remained were bare bones.

We had seen only a glimpse of the Egyptian vulture, which was overwhelmed by the larger more powerful white-rumped and

Himalayan griffon vulture. Up in the Himalaya we had a unique opportunity to see them at their soaring best. We'd hooked up with a small company in Pokhara that had been rescuing injured birds of prey for many years. A few years before they'd run out of money to keep their birds, and while they were frantically searching for ways to make some cash, discovered that you could go paragliding with the vultures! It all seemed a bit far-fetched to me, until I found myself launching off a high Himalayan peak underneath a parachute, and saw the white plumage of an Egyptian vulture coursing around my ears!

Paragliders read the signs in the world around them in order to soar. As the hills heat up in the sun, dark areas of rock, ploughed fields and roads heat up more quickly than other areas, creating pillars of rising hot air. If you fly into these thermals, the rising air will carry you aloft as well.

VULTURES UNDER THREAT

One of the most pressing concerns in world conservation is that facing the vultures of Asia and Africa. It sounds unbelievable, but in Asia they have declined by more than ninety-five per cent in recent years, due to the use of a veterinary drug called Diclofenac. It's fed to cattle as an anti-inflammatory, and when they die the vultures eat the carcass and overdose on the Diclofenac. It's a critical situation, not merely because these birds are so wondrous, but because they have such an essential role to play in the ecosystem, clearing up decaying carcasses and preventing the spread of disease. India has banned veterinary use of the drug, but illegal use continues. Without urgent action, these birds will never more be seen soaring above the cliff faces of the Himalaya.

The birds though are much more adept at finding and riding these thermals. With their insanely acute eyesight they can pick out a decaying carcass from a couple of kilometres away. They can also pinpoint the faintest rustle in the trees below that might indicate the start of a thermal, or tiny insects or flecks of dust borne aloft by the air currents. They head straight for them, and thus can be carried heavenwards with no expenditure of energy whatsoever.

It was a rare thrill – having the mighty Himalaya below me, actually getting higher and higher, and having the vulture scorch past almost contemptuously, occasionally coming to land on my hand and take proffered chunks of meat. His ease on the wing made me feel pathetically cumbersome, but showed in no uncertain terms why this high-altitude soarer was worthy of a place on the Deadly list.

ASIAN ONE-HORNED RHINOCEROS (*Rhinoceros unicornis*)

This rhino is not a predator, but known for having a grumpy nature due to being myopic (having poor vision) although its smell and hearing

are acute. Startling a one-horned rhino often results in a charge, though they'll bite rather than ram with their horn. We encountered these prehistoric creatures alongside the river in swampy reed beds, which is surprising as these are the most aquatic of all rhino species.

GIANT ASIAN HONEYBEES (*Apis dorsata*)

These weren't insects we intended to film in Nepal, as they tend to live on big cliff faces or trees, and we didn't have time to set it all up. However, as we were driving through a small village, I noticed many nests hanging off the balconies of the houses. It seemed they were encouraged to take up residence there so people could gather their honey. They're actually pretty docile, and like all bees, will only attack if you give them cause to think you might do them harm. Moving slowly and smoothly around their nests, we managed to film for an hour close enough to touch the nests without anyone being stung. As the series was in the home straight, we were ticking off animals trying to get to sixty. To find and film one as easily as this was a real bonus!

On an Asian elephant, looking for the one-horned rhino.

We discover a giant Asian honeybee nest on a family home in Nepal.

MUGGER (*Crocodylus palustris*)

The mugger or marsh crocodile is named after the Urdu word for water monster, and not because it steals handbags (!). They're the most common species of croc on the Indian subcontinent, but still manage to stay hidden from most people's view, spending a good deal of time in long burrows – and keeping their bodies immersed below the waterline. They will take larger mammal prey, but are generally shy of people, and very rarely a danger to us.

Mugger crocodile.

ASIAN ELEPHANT (*Elephas maximus*)

I feel a little guilty about putting Asian elephants on the list, as ninety-nine per cent of the time when you encounter them they are as placid

I meet a herd of Asian elephants.

and docile as kittens. However, this did give me an opportunity to talk about a very interesting facet of elephant life: musth. Musth is the condition that bull elephants get into when their hormones are raging and they really want to find a female. When in this state, they can become enraged and sometimes very dangerous. In Nepal we had a huge male in musth stomp towards us, and our guides (who had been as cool as you like in front of rhino, tiger and buffalo) could not get out of the area quickly enough. It turned out that same elephant had killed three people in previous weeks.

BEAKED SEA SNAKE (*Enhydrina schistosa*)

Sea snakes are to me completely fascinating. They have one elongated lung that runs most of the length of their body, enabling them to stay

Filming a sea snake.

underwater for extended periods of time, but still have to come to the surface to breathe. Their tail has become flattened and paddle-shaped, helping them swim through the water with whipping, sinuous movements. They also have some of the most potent of all venoms, due to the need to quickly paralyse fast-swimming, slippery fish, but are loath to bite in defence, so are little or no danger to humans.

RUSSELL'S VIPER (*Daboia russelii*)

The central premise of this series is animals that are deadly in their own world, and I am very loath to include animals because they are dangerous to us. Unfortunately you cannot talk about the Russell's viper without mentioning that it is a threat to human beings. It's probably the most dangerous snake to humans, not because it's a

Observing a Russell's viper - with great care.

mean or irascible serpent, but because its hunting strategy brings it into conflict with us. The snake comes into rice paddies in search of the rodents that live there. It lies in wait, perfectly disguised, and strikes at anything warm-blooded that comes close. This is often a human being, and as the people here live far from hospital and perhaps can't afford medical care, they don't receive treatment. Because of all these factors, Sri Lanka has the unpleasant statistic of being the country with the highest number of snakebite deaths (per head of population) every year.

INDIAN ROCK PYTHON (*Python molurus*)

The Indian python is one of the world's serpent giants. They are said to grow up to six metres in length, and like all such massive snakes, constrict or crush the life out of their prey. Constriction is generally thought to prevent a prey animal from breathing, but it is not always so simple. In many cases the victim dies from having all their internal organs squished – simply put, their organs burst! In other cases the nerves, arteries and veins that feed and emerge from the heart are blocked off. It is

An Indian rock python.

a risky method of killing though, as the snake has to keep hold of its struggling prey until it dies – not too bad if it's a rabbit, but a little more dangerous if it's a crocodile!

LEOPARD (*Panthera pardus*)

Leopards in Sri Lanka are unusual. Throughout most of their range, they live in the same places as larger carnivores such as tigers and lions, even hyenas. This means that when a leopard makes a kill it generally has to drag it up a tree to protect it. Here in Sri Lanka however, the leopard is top cat. Because of this leopards have evolved to fill the niche normally filled by tigers. They are the biggest of all leopards, feed happily on the ground and are less reclusive than other populations of leopard, which makes this the best spot in the world to see them!

Finding leopard tracks, which eventually led us to the largest leopards on Earth!

BLUE WHALE (*Balaenoptera musculus*)

Even four years ago, when we started to film Deadly, if I'd suggested to the crew that we film blue whales I'd have been laughed out of town. They may be the largest animal that's ever known to have lived, but they're rare, they live far out to sea, and even when you chance upon one they are at the surface for seconds before they disappear and pop up again kilometres away. Filming them would take months of effort, and a whole lot of luck. Just a few years ago, though, legendary underwater cameraman Simon Enderby got a quiet word from one of his scientist contacts that a population of blue whales was living off the coast of Sri Lanka pretty much all year round.

Just filming the whales was going to be tough enough, but we'd applied to the Sri Lankan government for special permits that would allow us to film the whales underwater, one of the biggest challenges we have ever taken on.

The first day out on the water gave us little cause for hope. Waves were high, and the boat was hurled about all over the place. We saw quite a few whales, some of them just metres from the boat, but poor Johnny simply had no chance to get a decent shot, and there was no way we were going to get into the water. That evening we retired to our hotel all feeling as if we'd taken on an impossible task. No roughing it for us this time though – we stayed alongside honeymooning couples at a charming hotel right on one of the beaches. I did my nightly exercises by the crashing surf, and we ate grilled prawns the size of lobster for dinner; very occasionally my job seems almost like a holiday! The second morning of filming, and we came down to the docks just after dawn. There was no wind, and the swell looked negligible. This was our big chance.

The reason blue whales have chosen to spend their year in this part of the Indian Ocean is uncertain. Blue whales mostly feed on a small crustacean called krill, which occurs in massive shoals or blooms. Krill are most common in Arctic seas, with an estimated five hundred million tonnes of them in the Southern Ocean alone, but are much less common as you head into tropical waters. One theory as to why blue whales are doing so well here in Sri Lanka is that a deep-sea trench running close to the shore has strong currents sweeping its depths and bringing nutrients up into shallower seas. These feed plankton, which feed the krill, which feed the whales.

There was no doubt that the whales here were feeding on krill. Just an hour or so into our search, we found a slick of orange goo on the surface of the sea. We hauled in a bucket, and it was like neon orange paste, stinking of sour seafood . . . blue whale poo! At least one whale had surfaced somewhere nearby within the last few minutes.

Blue whale underwater, gulp feeding.

How on earth we'd go about getting into the water with the whales we had no idea. All we could do was listen to the crew of our boat, and the scientists who had given us as much information as possible. Their advice was that it would be pointless to try to chase the whales; they cruise at 32 km/h, and if they feel herded they simply dive. Instead, we needed to watch them, try to figure out their rhythms and plop ourselves into the water well ahead of them, hoping they would swim past us. It was a gamble, and it seemed we would need phenomenal luck on our side in order to succeed.

Something that *was* on our side was visibility. A huge pod of spinner dolphins started playing around us, perhaps as many as a hundred dolphins, leaping and twisting and riding in our bow wave. Johnny and I decided to drop in to try out our filming equipment. The water was so clear that it was like hanging in space. The 'viz' (visibility, how far you can see underwater) was breathtaking. I watched fascinated as the dolphins played and frolicked deep deep beneath me. If we could get even within fifty metres of a whale, we'd be able to get a shot.

The whales were around us often, but generally too far off to be worth going after. Halfway through the afternoon though we picked up one whale who was surfacing close to us. He was keeping a regular pattern, diving for eight to nine minutes, then popping up for two or three minutes. The Sri Lankan crew had brought out a small RIB (rigid inflatable boat) with an outboard motor, and every time he popped up, the driver would pound over the waves, heading to where he guessed the whale might surface.

Bouncing over the waves, holding on to my underwater camera for dear life, using my coccyx as a pillow was honestly the most pain I've been through in order to get a shot. Inevitably though, we'd get into place and drop into the water just as the whale dived. I would power forwards with my free-diving fins on till I could fin no more, and would see little more than a glimpse of disappearing shadow. We were all beginning to think it simply was a step too far.

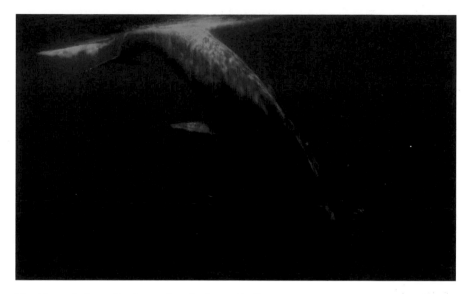

The blue whale - the largest animal on Earth.

Finally, towards the end of the day, a whale popped up alongside the RIB, and Johnny and I slipped over the side. We finned like crazy towards the line that it seemed our whale must take. Nothing. Just empty seas around us. I gasped and blew into my snorkel with the exertion, absolutely spent. And then out of the deep blue cruised an even deeper blue shape. The whale was heading straight at us. Just before drawing level with me, it flipped its tail flukes into the air, dropped its snout, and powered vertically downwards. I quickly breathed out as hard as possible, trying to rid my system of toxic carbon dioxide, then dragged in as much air as I could, and dived alongside it.

The blue whale is the largest animal on Earth, and bigger than any dinosaur we have yet discovered. They can weigh one hundred and eighty tonnes, and be thirty metres in length. That's pretty close to the measurements of a jumbo jet. Their tongue is as heavy as an elephant. They can eat as much as four tonnes of krill a day, which means they are the hungriest of all animals, and they have an aorta that a child could swim down. Their subsonic calls are said to travel over thousands of kilometres, and are among the loudest noises in nature, registering one hundred and eighty decibels; about the same as a stun grenade. This is an animal record-breaker, the great icon of the oceans, and an animal that is only recently returning from the brink of extinction. To see one in its own deep blue world is about as special as wildlife encounters get.

As I thrashed my fins, holding my camera ahead of me, I swam through the trail of bubbles created by the sweep of its vast tail flukes, and for a moment found myself alongside a diving blue whale. I continued down as far as possible, but already my lungs were screaming for air. Hanging in mid-water, I trained the camera on the whale as it powered into the depths, probably to begin feeding at around one hundred metres below the surface. I came up to the surface utterly ecstatic. We'd achieved the impossible. I'd got an underwater shot of a blue whale. Shuddering with effort and excitement, Johnny and I headed back to the main boat and, taut with anticipation, opened up the cameras to review the footage. I was hoping for whoops and yells from the crew, but instead everyone nodded politely and told us, 'Well done'. Truth was, Johnny had been too far away to get a good shot, and my shot was out of focus for the first half. The challenge had beaten us. Johnny and I both went and sat on our own in different parts of the boat, too heartbroken to talk to anyone. We stayed out until the light was almost gone, an exhausting eleven hours at sea in blistering sunshine.

Next day, I decided to take a different tack, and not to use the RIB. I was so battered and bruised that it felt as if I'd done ten rounds with the heavyweight champion of the world (which in a way I guess I had!). Also, it seemed that the whales didn't like the noisy engines of the RIB, but seemed quite relaxed with the main boat. We were essentially putting all our faith in the hope that a whale would simply pop up alongside us. This was perhaps an even bigger gamble, as we wouldn't be able to manoeuvre into position, but one that ultimately paid off. Big time.

It was midday before we even saw a whale, but for the next few hours there were always whales in view. Their blowholes exhaled water vapour and 'bad' gases (just like me blowing off carbon dioxide) up to nine metres in the air, so you could see them from miles away. At about 2.00 pm our plan came good. A whale surfaced a hundred metres off to our port side, we cut the motors and Johnny and I bailed straight over. This time we didn't fin, but just hung in the water and hoped. Then suddenly there it was. Like a vast submarine, barely seeming to be moving, it cruised towards us, surfaced to breathe, bending its spine like a bow before dropping its snout again.

Scanning the sea for blue whales.

I sensed it would come up once more before diving, so swam behind Johnny, all the time deep-breathing to try to oxygenate my blood. Then as the whale made to dive, I went down too. Later on, watching Johnny's stunning footage, we were to see the largest animal on Earth,

Swimming with a blue whale.

in perfect crystal clear detail (and in focus, Johnny was keen to point out!) moving with hypnotically relaxed swooshes of a tail that was as broad as a minibus. It nosed into the depths like a vanishing nuclear submarine, and then at the last moment, a tiny anchovy swims into shot, dwarfed by this leviathan god of the oceans. It's me. I just managed to get a shot of those gargantuan tail flukes as they swept in front of my face, before beginning the long swim up to the surface. Nick, Johnny and I, who between us have seen a fair amount of what the natural world has to offer, agreed that it had been the greatest wildlife encounter of our lives. By this point I hadn't had a day not working in months and months, and was near exhaustion, but finishing the penultimate filming trip of the series with such a mammoth success made us all feel we'd be ending on a real high.

FLORIDA

EASTERN DIAMONDBACK RATTLESNAKE

(*Crotalus adamanteus*)

There's something very special about rattlers. The chilling sound of their warning rattle (the soundtrack of many an old cowboy movie) and evil-looking faces belie the fact that actually they're one of the easiest venomous snakes to handle. I've caught more than twenty species around the Americas, but had never seen the daddy of them all, the Eastern diamondback.

Florida was the perfect place to wrap up this long series. The Everglade swamps, and the surrounding dry forests, are some of the most exciting wild places in America, and home to some of the most dramatic wildlife. We were here in the spring, when many rattlers emerge from their winter sleep. They're not very active, and can be hard to find, so we teamed up with Dr Bruce Means, a legendary herpetologist (reptile/amphibian scientist). He had encouraged several snakes to swallow small radio transmitters before they went into hibernation, and had a rough idea of where they would be. All we had to do was go out with a receiver, and that would lead us straight to the snakes. Theoretically.

In actual fact, we picked up a signal straight away, but just could not find the snakes! We narrowed the source of the signal down to a patch of scrub no bigger than a tennis court, yet still spent hours scouring it to no avail. As usual with these searches, the first hour or so I am on high alert, expecting to find a snake under every branch, then the excitement starts to wane, before eventually I start believing I'll never find anything! I was at just this stage when we finally found our champion, a hefty male who was as thick as my arm, and a healthy metre and a half long. As I approached, he let rip with that rattle, to me one of the most exciting sounds on Earth.

Every time the snake moults, the skin leaves behind a cusp of old, brittle skin. Over the years, this builds up into an instrument which is shaken like a maraca by one of the fastest-moving muscles in the vertebrate world. Any animal – regardless of whether they've seen a rattler before – instantly knows to leave this snake well alone. This is a mechanism designed to frighten away predators, as is the hood of the cobra and the hiss of all reptiles, and far from being aggressive, it is a display of fear. The snake hopes that by making lots of noise and making itself seem scary, it can avoid conflict.

An Eastern diamondback rattlesnake.

This is borne out when you pick up a rattlesnake. They very rarely strike, and will hang on a snake hook perfectly balanced. With this particular snake, I had to hold the hook with both hands; the snake was SO heavy! I pinned the head to expose the fangs; over two centimetres long, hinged so they can lie against the upper jaw, dripping beads of dark yellow venom that would stop a rabbit moving in less than a minute.

A closer look at a rattlesnake's fangs.

We'd brought along a thermal-imaging camera, which sees the world in heat, rather than light. Originally I'd planned to use it to demonstrate how pit vipers 'see' their prey, with the heat-detecting pits in their face. However, the snake was really cold after a chilly spring night, so I decided to try a little experiment. Everyone thinks of snakes as being cold-blooded, but this is not the full story. The more complete biological terms are 'ectothermic', which means getting heat from outside its body, or 'poikilothermic', a right mouthful that means that an animal tracks the ambient temperature and lets its body go through a broad range of temperatures. We mammals tend to keep our core temperature at a toasty 38°C.

My snake right now was maybe 5°C or 6°C. With the thermal camera rolling, I placed him on a piece of old metal sheet lying near to Bruce's backwoods shack. We'd already found several other snakes underneath the metal, gathering there to increase the speed and efficiency of their basking. As we watched on the thermal camera, our rattler (dark blue as it was still cold) started to turn green, then orange, then red as the heat from the sun and the metal warmed its blood. When it had reached a nice warm 34°C, the snake lazily slithered off, having gathered enough warmth to drive its metabolism and give it the energy to hunt. No nearby rat or rabbit would be safe.

Rattlesnake in position for our thermal camera.

RATTLESNAKE ROUND-UP

Rattlesnakes very rarely harm humans, unless they are deliberately harassed by people who don't know what they are doing (which happens more than it should). They are extremely important animals and play a valuable role in keeping pest rodents and rabbits in check, but many people don't understand this and fear the snakes. Sadly, this leads to many being collected and killed in their hundreds of thousands in annual 'rattlesnake round-ups'. Here snakes are dumped in pits, skinned alive, burned, turned into belts and boots and killed so their rattles can be put on to necklaces or hats. These events have been going on since 1939, and are having a devastating effect on the numbers and top size of rattlers in the States.

VENUS FLYTRAP (*Dionaea muscipula*)

The next day couldn't have been more different. We wandered out into damp meadows close to where we'd been filming rattlers, in search of only the second plant to feature on Deadly 60. Perhaps the most extraordinary thing about Venus flytraps is that these snappy shrubs seem to be able to count. If the hairs inside them are touched simultaneously, or two separate hairs are touched within a few seconds then the trap snaps shut, encasing an insect inside. Digestive enzymes break the insect down, and the plant uses the resulting nutrients to grow.

Looking for carnivorous plants.

BOBCAT *(Lynx rufus)*

Closely related to the lynx, the bobcat is a widespread and successful predator. We put a radio collar on this particular cat so scientists could track its movements and learn as much as possible about the extent of its range. Bobcats can leap as much as three metres to catch prey like hares and rabbits, and are lightning quick when they need to be.

Attaching a radio collar to an anaesthetised bobcat.

DOLPHINS

(Tursiops truncatus)

Some bottlenose dolphins have picked up a remarkable behaviour known as 'mud ringing'. A group herds mullet in very shallow water. One swims around them turned on its side, thrashing the mud with its tail, forming a murky pen around the fish. The mullets' escape strategy is to leap out of the ring, and right into the waiting mouths of the other dolphins, whose heads are out of the water ready to gulp down dinner.

Bottlenose dolphins feeding on mullet.

COTTONMOUTH (*Agkistrodon piscivorus*)

In the swamplands of the US lurks a venomous viper with an unexpectedly wide gape, and superb swimming skills; the cottonmouth. Its scientific name means 'fish-eater', and though the cottonmouth will eat frogs, birds and other waterside creatures, fish are certainly its food of choice. Finding venomous snakes is always a challenge; they are never as numerous or as obvious as people expect. We caught our cottonmouth after a few days in the spookiest of swamps; a nervy, but thrilling experience.

Cottonmouth snake.

FIRE ANTS (*Solenopsis geminata*)

Apart from human beings, most animals live in a sort of harmony with their natural environment. If they're suddenly relocated to an unfamiliar habitat, though, it can be a different story. Invasive red fire ants are making their way across the States after being brought in accidentally with shipments of plants. They're predatory, and can make a right mess of local ecosystems. They also sting. After delving around in a nest to show how aggressive they can be, my fingers came up in black pustules, and still showed scars months later.

Filming the cast of a fire ant nest.

ALLIGATORS (*Alligator mississippiensis*)

In the southern states of America, one ancient reptile is making a spectacular comeback. Like all the crocodilians, alligators have been severely persecuted over the years. People have hunted them through fear and for their skin, which is used to make things like belts and boots. However, once hunting was prohibited throughout much of their range, they boomed. There are now as many as a million gators in Florida alone, so that's where we decided to try and swim with them.

An American alligator.

The crew and I took a boat out at night in the swamp to find our first gators. Usually I don't bother trying for crocs by day; they're too wary, and impossibly well camouflaged. At night though they give themselves away with eyeshine. Like many animals that conduct much of their deadly business in the dark, they have a layer of cells at the back of the eye called the *tapetum lucidum* (Latin for 'bright tapestry'), which reflects light back through the retina, intensifying their night vision. This has the side effect of making their eyes shine fiery red in a spotlight. Sometimes when out in good gator country at night, it's as if a hundred fireflies spring into light with every sweep of the torch. Usually the gators are dazzled by the beam, and you can approach to within a metre or so before they duck underwater. Tonight though was strange. The gators were freakishly nervous. They disappeared when we were still far away, and we barely got a glimpse of them. The local guides were unanimous; 'You get in the water, them gators gonna disappear. You ain't gonna see 'em for dust.' It seemed they had a point.

Gators are the most vocal of all crocodilians, and the males bellow when they're in a mating mood. Much of the sound is too low for human ears to hear, but the audible sounds reverberate up through the water, and all the other males in the area join in. During the breeding season, they slap their heads on the water, get seriously territorial, and don't take kindly to anything that might appear to be competition. We were in Florida in April, right in the middle of breeding time. I'm guessing that was the reason for what happened next.

The location we'd chosen was a stunning river system fed by subterranean springs. The water was so clear that even from the boat I could see the freckles on the flanks of the spotted garfish beneath us, and the colour of the eyes of red-eared turtles swimming through the river plants. Cruising past ghostly white cypress trees drooping with Spanish moss was like taking a trip back in time. That seemed particularly weird as just ten minutes before we'd been cruising past burger joints and theme parks on Florida highways; this place was a hidden gem.

The cameraman and I both kitted up, chatting with each other about safety and how we would watch each other's backs. We made out that we were relaxed and totally cool with it all, but secretly our hearts were going a hundred beats a minute – after all, we were about to get in the water with alligators! We were going to be free-diving, so didn't have cumbersome tanks, just mask and fins, plus cameras in waterproof housings. Free-diving fins are longer and stiffer than normal, so we can cruise with just the slightest movements of our feet; ideal for conserving energy and not spooking animals.

Ever so quietly, we slipped off the side of the boat and into the water. Once under it was so clear that we seemed to be flying. We'd all pretty much got used to the idea that we wouldn't succeed in seeing a gator, but the river was so beautiful that we decided to do some filming anyway. The springs were impossibly deep blue holes that apparently went hundreds, perhaps thousands, of metres down into the Earth. No fishing was allowed on the river, so the water was literally bursting

An alligator lurking in the swamps.

Filming alligators in the swamps.

with life; dozens of species of fish, common snapping turtles and along the river's edge three species of heron, plus cormorants and anhinga, or snake-necked, birds. The whole place looked like a film set, and in a way it kind of was – as early Tarzan and Bond movies had been filmed against the backdrop of these mystical swamps.

After one breath-hold dive, I came to the surface to get some air and turned back to the main boat where the rest of the crew were filming. I started to do a piece to camera about how we'd have to give up on getting a shot of a gator in its watery world, when Kirstine, the director, shouted, 'Steve! There's a gator swimming straight towards you!'

This is the oldest trick in the book. When nothing's happening, the crew often play jokes, and the 'Look out it's behind you!' line is an old favourite. However, I decided to humour her, and turned around.

An alligator *was* swimming lazily in my direction. It was difficult to get a sense of how big the thing was from the surface, so I breathed out, sank to the bottom of the river and looked up. The gator was about two metres, longer than I am tall, and plenty big enough to do damage. Just then he made a move, twitching visibly sideways to bring his nose straight towards me. He started swimming with more purpose, broad paddle-shaped tail driving him on easy and fast. I'd been trying to keep my heart rate down, as it helps your free-diving, but suddenly it was beating fit to burst out of my ears. I recalled the statistics. Alligators very rarely attack people, but the ones that have done are comparatively small . . . around about two metres long in fact.

He stopped swimming and hung ominously in front of me, kept buoyant by the air in his lungs. The five-clawed feet dangled down beneath his body. I could see that characteristic broad snout, and teeth spilling out of his closed mouth. The second thing that crossed my mind was that gators attack large prey at the surface, but are not known for doing so when submerged. If only I'd had some scuba tanks! However, I didn't, so I breathed out and sank to the bottom again. The gator cruised over the top of me, silhouetted beautifully against the sun.

The crew were scared stiff. They couldn't see me, and this scary-looking beast was hovering above me, just eyes and nostrils breaking the surface. As I watched transfixed, the gator sank. It was incredible, like watching a submarine go down. Crocs have a special organ called the diaphramaticus, which enables them to push their lungs back, compressing and shifting them around the organs inside the body cavity, altering their buoyancy. They also swallow stones called gastroliths, which may be kept in their stomachs to be used as ballast, enabling them to sink like . . . well, like a stone. There was not so much as a bubble from his nostrils as he dived.

On the bottom of the river, the gator was a totally different animal. He allowed me to free-dive right alongside him, close enough to run my hands down his velvety sides if I'd wanted to. I used my underwater camera to film his scaly tail and eyes in super-close-up. He peered at me through the nictitating membrane, a third eyelid which functions almost like a pair of swimming goggles, protecting the eye underwater. After maybe ten minutes (with me diving down repeatedly, coming back up to the surface to breathe) he gently moved off into cover. He could easily have stayed down there on the bottom for many hours if he'd chosen to, dropping his heart rate to just a few beats a minute, and barely requiring any oxygen.

My view of the inquisitive gator.

Looking back on it later, when the red mist had cleared, I certainly don't think that the alligator had any intention of eating me. Instead he was issuing a challenge. He was a male who saw me as a rival, and wanted to see if this strange intruder would back down. When I didn't, he assumed I was a worthy adversary, and went on his way. Maybe things would have been different if I hadn't been wearing my long free-diving fins, which made me look bigger. I'm not sure. I do know that this unforgettable prehistoric encounter in the swamps of the Deep South was a very fitting way to finish a phenomenal series.

DEADLY ... DONE!

Sixty species, six continents and six months on the road filming . . .
If I had to choose my highlights then it would have to be alligators,
blue whales and speedy sailfish, but it would be hard to ignore the
mighty scolopendra, or being bounced underneath a helicopter
and lowered on to a crocodile's nest! That was certainly Graham's
big moment, Nick and Johnny are with me on the whales and
Smiley Simon was particularly bowled over by nearly being eaten
by a Komodo dragon!

It's been a grand adventure, but it's not done yet. My crew may be a
tight little clan, but hopefully you see yourselves as part of the family.
The Deadly ethos is to encourage you all to see the wild world around
you with fresh eyes, filled with delight and wonder. We want you to
discover the deadly mini-beasts hunting in your own back garden.
You are hereby charged to watch the kestrels and buzzards hovering
over the motorway verges, and listen to the songbirds chanting
warnings of hunting pet cats and sparrowhawks. Learn to read the
stories left behind in the mud by animals that passed in the night,
and if you find a wildlife crime scene, see if you can play detective
and figure out whodunit!

Most importantly, it's down to you to do your bit to help the
threatened animals around the world. How about raising some
cash to save an endangered species or a local reserve, or perhaps
volunteering for a wildlife charity, or doing something to raise
awareness of a conservation issue?

This is my challenge to you.
Your Deadly mission has just begun . . .

INDEX

PICTURE CREDITS

(b: bottom; t: top; l: left; r: right; c: centre) 7, 21, 95, 97 Craig Adams 2012 (from Deadly 60 Series 3); 18, 160, 163, 165, 166, 167 Scott Alexander 2012 (from Deadly 60 Series 3); 23, 129, 130, 168, 172 Nick Allinson 2012 (from Deadly 60 Series 3); 15, 33, 35, 36, 37, 56, 57, 69t, 69b, 71, 73, 74, 103, 104, 105, 124, 125, 126, 146, 147, 149, 154, 155b, 156t, 156b, 159t, 159b, 170, 179, 181, 182, 191b, 192t, 192b, 199 © BBC 2012; 12, 144t Jesus A Vergara Castro 2012 (from Deadly 60 Series 3); 22, 28, 42, 44, 46, 48, 60, 62, 67, 70, 77b, 79, 120, 132, 134, 193 Kirstine Davidson 2012 (from Deadly 60 Series 3); 10, 30 Emily Duggan 2012 (from Deadly 60 Series 3); 14, 80, 83, 86, 88, 90, 92, 99t, 99b, 100, 107, 108, 110, 117, 119, 136, 142, 143, 144b, 145, 150, 151, 155t Katy Elson 2012 (from Deadly 60 Series 3); 133 Simon Enderby 2012 (from Deadly 60 Series 3); 141 Saul Gutierrez 2012 (from Deadly 60 Series 3); 87, 89, 101, 106, 112, 114 171, 173, 174, 175 Ruth Harries 2012 (from Deadly 60 Series 3); 52, 53 Kate Horvath 2012 (from Deadly 60 Series 3); 38, 39, 138, 152, 157, 158 Graham MacFarlane 2012 (from Deadly 60 Series 3); 27, 184, 188, 189, 190, 197 Bruce Means 2012 (from Deadly 60 Series 3); 127t & 127b,128t, 128b 183 Johnny Rogers 2012 (from Deadly 60 Series 3); 123 Ernesto Contreras Ruiz 2012 (from Deadly 60 Series 3); 50, 54 Rich Stevenson 2012 (from Deadly 60 Series 3); 45, 58, 59, 77t, 191t, 194, 196 Elizabeth Sutton 2012 (from Deadly 60 Series 3);

Ardea: 16 Ferrero-Labat; 17t Suzi Eszterhas; 40 Jean Paul Ferrero; 66, 187 Pat Morris; 84 Adrian Warren; 177 Doc White; **Shutterstock:** 43 Madlen; 91 Pedro Salaverria

Every effort has been made to contact the copyright holders but if there are any omissions, please contact the Publishers, who will be happy to correct in future editions.

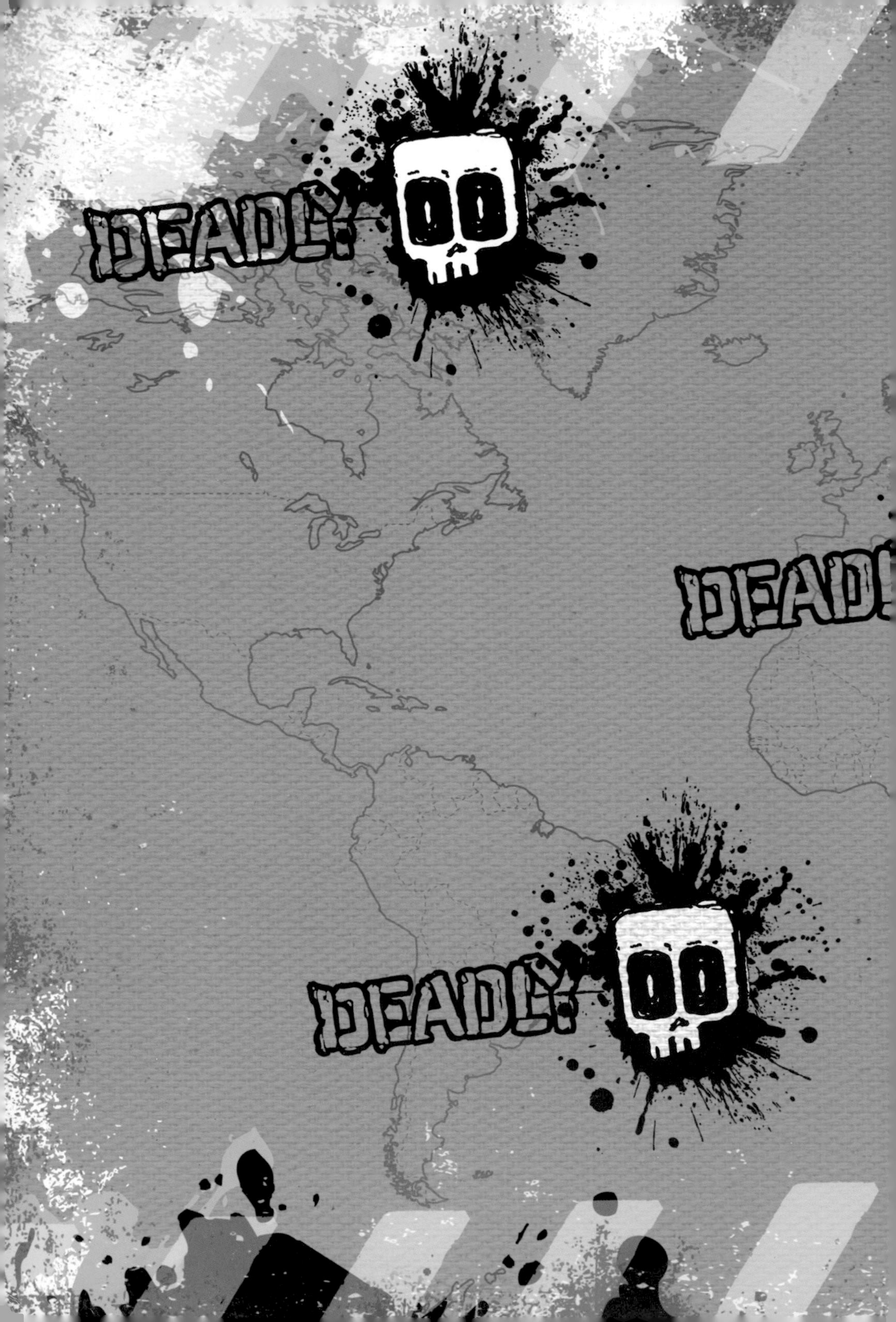
DEADLY
DEADLY
DEADLY